The Funny Shap

Devotions for the Rest of Us

here
we
stand

THE FUNNY SHAPE OF FAITH
Devotions for the Rest of Us

Scripture quotations are from the New Revised Standard Version Bible, copyright © 1989 by the Division of Christian Education of the National Council of the Churches of Christ in the USA. Used by permission. All rights reserved.

Martin Luther quotation on page 233 is from *The Life of Luther Written by Himself,* M. Michelet, ed. (London: G. Bell and Sons, Publishers, 1904).

Martin Luther quotation on page 253 is from "Out of the Depths I Cry to You," *Lutheran Book of Worship,* Hymn 295. Text: Martin Luther, 1483-1546; tr. Gracia Grindal, b. 1943. © 1978 *Lutheran Book of Worship.*

Martin Luther quotation on page 275 is from *Commentary on Peter and Jude,* John Nicholas Lenker, ed. (Grand Rapids: Kregel Classics, Publishers, 1990).

Martin Luther quotations on pages 87, 91, 123, 125, 241, 243, 245, 255, 257, 269, 285, and 291 are from *The Book of Concord: The Confessions of the Evangelical Lutheran Church,* Tappert, T. G., ed. (Philadelphia: Fortress Press, 1959).

Martin Luther quotations on pages 81, 99, 107, 109, 137, 141, 143, 175, 177, 183, 191, and 239 are from *Luther's Works,* vols. 27, 47, 44, 52, 48, 30, 32, 54, 54, 4, 51, and 35, respectively. J. J. Pelikan, H. C. Oswald, and H. T. Lehmann, eds. (Saint Louis: Concordia Publishing House and Philadelphia: Fortress Press, 1958-1974).

ISBN 978-0-8066-5761-5

New brand development editor: Kristofer Skrade
Editors: Arlene Flancher and Laurie J. Hanson
Contributing writers: Lou Carlozo, Mark K. Johnson, Rebecca Ninke, Carla Thompson Powell, Darin Wiebe
Cover and book design: Michelle L. N. Cook
Illustrations: John Bush

The paper used in this publication meets the minimum requirements of American National Standard for Information Sciences—Permanence of Paper for Printed Library Materials, ANSI Z329.48-1984.

Manufactured in Canada

11   10   09   08   07   2   3   4   5   6   7   8   9   10

CONTENTS

CONTENTS

CONTENTS

CONTENTS

CONTENTS

A Note from the Publisher

We at Augsburg Fortress are blessed to have worked with John Bush.

I knew John for several years before he started cartooning for Augsburg Fortress. In fact, John was my neighbor. I'd see him out and about with his kids—carting them around in his minivan, stopping to chat with folks along the way. You could say our neighborhood was John's office. It was where he got his material. At the coffee shop or supermarket or filling up his van, it is where John ingeniously observed and commented on the funny shape of ordinary life.

Indeed John Bush was a gift of God to this world. For those of us who worked with John, one of our highlights was when he would bring in his new batch of cartoons. They would always liven our hearts—and still do.

As you read this book, I hope you see how this unique weave of Scripture, prayer, and wit come alive as devotion. Read it, share it, and laugh out loud. My friend John would want nothing more.

—Bill Huff

Foreword

John Bush was a freelance cartoonist for nearly thirty years, working primarily with business/training/Fortune 500 companies in the Minneapolis, Minnesota, area.

Although he never wore his faith "on his sleeve," John had a strong respect for and understanding of the Bible. He knew it, and he lived it. As an illustrator, John had the unique ability to create whimsical cartoons directly related to Scripture.

As a healthy young man of fifty-two, John was diagnosed with Stage 4 non-smoker's lung cancer in September 2005. In spite of the challenge ahead of him, he said, "I will fight with everything I have to live." He died in late July 2006.

This collection of John's work, *The Funny Shape of Faith: Devotions for the Rest of Us,* is a small sample of the work he did for Augsburg Fortress, Publishers. We are grateful that those at Augsburg Fortress see the value in John's work. Once again we share it with all of you.

—Nancy Jenkins Bush

Introduction

The Funny Shape of Faith isn't just another book of devotions. It's a book of faithful, fun, and fresh devotions.

That's right, faithful, fun, and fresh. Those words do go together! Here's how:

• **Faithful**—The artist and writers ground their work in the Bible and Christian beliefs.

• **Fun**—This book uses humor in ways that might bring a smile, a chuckle, or even an all-out belly laugh. It's not that we aren't serious about the Bible, faith, and Christian living. It's that the God who creates everything from aardvarks to zebras is a God of wonder and play, as well as a God of power and might. And the humans God creates think, say, and do things that seem outlandish, twisted, and downright funny when we stop to think about it. And sometimes, in the middle of a good laugh, we can learn something about ourselves, the world, and God.

• **Fresh**—When you combine faithfulness and fun, you get freshness, too. That's in the surprisingly refreshing, ice-cold-lemonade-on-a-hot-day sense of the word, and also in the edgy, I-can't-believe-you-said-that sense of the word. The surprise and the edginess can catch us off guard. They can also help us grow.

From cover to cover, *The Funny Shape of Faith* isn't just another book of devotions. It's devotions for you—and the rest of us.

Ten Things to Do with Your Faith

You Don't Need Frog's Legs
to Settle Your Uneasy Stomach

Now faith is the assurance of things hoped for,
the conviction of things not seen.
—Hebrews 11:1

Frogs are made for leaping, while humans don't seem quite as, well, springy. To us, a leap of faith can look like a solo bungee jump without a net—and who wants a crash landing?

But a leap of faith never takes us beyond the reach of God's loving arms. The God of the universe, who gives life and faith, is not going to abandon us during times of growth and challenge. God is with us all the way! That calls for leaping.

My Lord of leaping, I don't want to tiptoe. I don't want to run in place. Give me faith and let me leap! Amen.

In the Body of Christ,
Even Sore Thumbs Are Useful

For just as the body is one and has many members, and all the
members of the body, though many, are one body, so it is with Christ.
—1 Corinthians 12:12

Do Jesus' followers, also called "the body of Christ," have what
it takes to make a difference in the world? Well, think about this:
First, Jesus continues to live and breathe through us. Second, as
we act, the love of Christ spreads into new corners of the world.

We don't need the time and ambition of the guy with the dented
digits here. Mother Teresa, a humble woman who gave much of
her own life to help the poor, said we as Christians cannot do
great things, but little things with great love.

*Creator of the message, show me where I belong in the body
of Christ, and how my love, talents, and time can make your
amazing love real for others. Amen.*

As a Good Book, It's Great

All scripture is inspired by God and is useful for teaching,
for reproof, for correction, and for training in righteousness.
—2 Timothy 3:16

Sometimes it may seem like God is silent. But, for starters, the Bible tells us that creation began with a word from God. The Bible also tells us God's promises—for a future and a hope, for forgiveness and new life. Finally, the Bible tells us that Jesus is God's Word—in Jesus we can see and hear God.

God still speaks to us today through the Bible. Like the very best stories, you can read the Bible over and over again and hear something new each time. You don't need to be religious, just open up a Bible. Read. Listen. Repeat.

God who still speaks, thank you for your words that continue to ring true to this day. As I read the Bible, help me listen to you. Amen.

Turning Sinners into Winners

"For God so loved the world that he gave his only Son, so that everyone who believes in him may not perish but may have eternal life."
—John 3:16

Have we ever sinned? Of course. Will we sin again, despite our best intentions? No doubt about it. If sin were "fixed" by jumping through hoops, obeying all the rules, or going on a self-help binge and finding the ultimate diet and exercise program, we would always fall short.

But wait! Sin and fear don't have the last word here.

God loves the world. God loves us. God loves you. We fall short, but God's Son came into the world. And because Jesus died and rose again, we become part of an unending circle of love.

God of love and sacrifice, I am in awe of what you have done for me. Thank you for bringing me into your circle of love. Amen.

The Bird Meets the Word

And when Jesus had been baptized, just as he came up
from the water, suddenly the heavens were opened to him and
he saw the Spirit of God descending like a dove and alighting on him.
—Matthew 3:16

To be submerged under water is a threatening thing for those of us who are afraid of it . . . or can't swim. But at his baptism, Jesus foreshadows his own resurrection by going under and rising up again.

Then the Spirit of God descends. If we were to choose a bird that powerful, it might be a swift predator—a hawk or a condor. But instead, God's Spirit comes down "like a dove." It's not hard to imagine that Spirit saying something to the effect of, "Relax, I'm a bird of pray."

God of power and might, sometimes I see myself as a bird—very small, very frail—and yet you love me and call me your own. Let your love shine through me. Amen.

A New Wrinkle on Social Justice

Now we have received not the spirit of the world, but the Spirit that is from God, so that we may understand the gifts bestowed on us by God.
—1 Corinthians 2:12

Serving God and others—what a heavy load, an awesome responsibility. Maybe it helps to remember that we have gifts to help with the serving—gifts given to us, in this case, by God.

We can experience deep joy in using our gifts. But that would be only half the story if we didn't help others and enrich their lives. Serving God and others through our gifts is an adventure!

Lord of justice, thank you for my gifts—both those I have discovered and those I have yet to tap. Help me to honor you by growing these gifts and using them to help others in exciting, liberating ways. Amen.

Now Here's Food for Thought

Three times I appealed to the Lord about this, that it would leave me, but he said to me, "My grace is sufficient for you, for power is made perfect in weakness." So I will boast all the more gladly of my weaknesses, so that the power of Christ may dwell in me.
—2 Corinthians 12:8-9

The apostle Paul did a lot to spread the story of Jesus, but he wasn't a powerful or perfect person. He had weaknesses and faults just like the rest of us. He relied on God and others to live. He never could have done what he did on his own. That made it all the more clear that the great things he accomplished only happened because of God's power working in him.

God's power can be at work in someone who is weak, imperfect, and messed up—someone like us.

God who feeds and informs, I am weak, but you are strong. I can depend on you. Startle me with your power. Amen.

Are You Lost 'Cause of a Lost Cause?

... so shall my word be that goes out from my mouth;
it shall not return to me empty, but it shall accomplish that
which I purpose, and succeed in the thing for which I sent it.
—Isaiah 55:11

Where do we find words to move others when we feel tired, uninspired, unsure? What do we do when it feels like something is a "lost cause"? Well, there's good news here. Sharing the story of Jesus isn't our cause, it's God's. It's a message we bring to others as a gift, a message that can change the course of a day or a life.

And God is known for saving what we would call "lost causes."

Savior of lost causes, I need a sign—because mine is blank! Help me to share your timeless message of love, service, and truth. Let my banner point the way to you. Amen.

Don't Let Stewardship Go to the Dogs

Send out your bread upon the waters,
for after many days you will get it back.
—Ecclesiastes 11:1

A dog that sees a bowl or a plate will probably sniff if, lick it, and even try to eat out of it. (Any dog lover can confirm this.) Luckily, we're not ruled by instinct or impulse. But how do we respond when the plate comes by?

Maybe we think that once money leaves our hands, it's lost. Nothing could be further from God's truth. To begin with, our offering can bring results—whether it plants a garden in our community or aids children a world away. But there is more. Ask any people who give regularly and cheerfully and you're bound to hear story after story about how giving has made a difference in their lives and in their faith.

Giving God, when I feel like I don't have enough, remind me that you are a God of boundless abundance. Amen.

The Quality Time Quandary

So he set off and went to his father. But while he was still far off,
his father saw him and was filled with compassion; he ran
and put his arms around him and kissed him.
—Luke 15:20

Jesus tells a story about a wayward son. This son wastes his inheritance, finally comes to his senses, then stumbles home in utter defeat. We wouldn't be surprised if his father launched into a big lecture at this point. But instead, the father runs to his son, hugs him, kisses him, and throws a huge party!

This story offers encouragement to all of us who need "quality time" with God. God is in charge of the universe, but never too busy for us. Just as a parent hovers adoringly over a sleeping child, God stays in our midst. No matter how long we are absent or distracted or just plain rebellious, God greets us with nothing less than unbridled joy.

God of all time, there never seems to be enough time. But still, I need to spend time with you. I pray for your love and understanding, beyond anything I can imagine. Amen.

You'll Probably Be Surprised by Who Is at the Heavenly Banquet

Heaven: This Place Has No Class

"No slave can serve two masters; for a slave will either hate
the one and love the other, or be devoted to the one
and despise the other. You cannot serve God and wealth."
—Luke 16:13

It's not riches alone, but the blind pursuit of wealth that
"enslaves" a person. Money can help us do tremendous good for
others. But all who focus on getting more and more stuff are
caught in a vicious cycle. Like drugs, alcohol, or gambling, money
and stuff can be powerful addictions.

The powerful trap of pursuing wealth is always present in our
world. But Jesus is always present, too, and he is more powerful
than money and any stuff we can accumulate.

*Lord of rich, poor, and all creation, help me avoid the trap of
money and stuff. Break down the divides that separate people, and
help me see all people as your children. Amen.*

What If You Had a Party and Nobodies Came?

"Those slaves went out into the streets and gathered all whom they found, both good and bad; so the wedding hall was filled with guests."
—Matthew 22:10

The movie *Wedding Crashers* could have been based on this verse, except for one thing. The people "crashing" this party have invitations. They're replacements for the original no-show guests.

The party goes on. The hall is filled. Drink flows; maybe Jesus is turning water into wine again. It's a celebration, a holy ritual that takes place with both "good and bad" present.

"The good and the bad." We sure think we know the difference, don't we? But we are all capable of bad. It's a good thing God has invited us into the celebration.

Lord of nobodies, sometimes your "guest list" makes me really uncomfortable. Help me to reach out to others, as you reached out to me. Amen.

Those dealing with the poor must wash hands before returning to work.

CBUSH

What to Pour on Those Who Are Poor

On the last day of the festival, the great day, while Jesus
was standing there, he cried out, "Let anyone who is thirsty
come to me, and let the one who believes in me drink.
As the scripture has said, 'Out of the believer's heart
shall flow rivers of living water.'"
—John 7:37-38

As living water pours sustenance on us, so we pour it onto others.
It's not for wasting in the way rock stars empty bottled water into
bathtubs. We can't horde it; it can't be sold. It can only be given
away, just as Christ gave his life away for us (including those of
us who are poor or homeless).

Think what a little living water, showered with utmost care and
humility, can do for someone who is thirsty. Think about what it
has done for you.

*Protector of people in need, make me a vessel to pour out love,
mercy, and compassion to those parched for it. Amen.*

Cleanup Time

Then Peter began to speak to them: "I truly understand that God shows
no partiality, but in every nation anyone who fears him
and does what is right is acceptable to him."
—Acts 10:34-35

Think of all the effort and energy wasted on trying to label and
oppress those who are different.

God doesn't play this game. God simply loves. And, try as we
might, that love can't be confined to anything less than all
creation. Whatever your skin color, gender, IQ, age, income, or
past, you are invited to the heavenly banquet.

*God of the clean, unclean, and all in between, help me to leave
labels behind and see only fellow humans, brothers and sisters in
Christ. Amen.*

When the Tough Get Going, the Going Gets Tough

My brothers and sisters, whenever you face trials of any kind, consider it nothing but joy, because you know that the testing of your faith produces endurance; and let endurance have its full effect, so that you may be mature and complete, lacking in nothing.

—James 1:2-4

It's very tempting to run away and hide from situations that seem too tough for us. Trials are "nothing but joy"? Is James some kind of nut?

When we come face to face with someone or something bigger than we are, we're tempted to turn tail and run right now.

We can consider those tough times joys only because God is always with us.

God, when I run into people or situations that seem too big for me, remind me that you are always with me. Amen.

Beware of Identity Theft

So if anyone is in Christ, there is a new creation: everything old has passed away; see, everything has become new!
—2 Corinthians 5:17

One way to become a new person is to make like Prince and fashion a persona, the way stars pluck duds from a wardrobe. This is not what happened to Saul.

The followers of Jesus were afraid of Saul, and for good reason! Saul had made a name for himself by persecuting the early Christians, tracking them down, and hauling them off to prison.

But Jesus turned Saul's life around (read about this in Acts 9). Paul, formerly known as Saul, began spreading the good news about Jesus and doing great things for the church. This 180-degree change in direction was a total transformation only God could pull off.

Name above all names, forgive my sins and make me new every day. Amen.

Lost: Soul. Reward: Eternal Life.

"Which one of you, having a hundred sheep and losing one of them,
does not leave the ninety-nine in the wilderness and go
after the one that is lost until he finds it?"
—Luke 15:4

Your typical "lost and found" at a bus station, shopping mall, or sports arena consists of junky trinkets, hats, gloves, and old toys, all piled in a bent cardboard box, never to be claimed.

Heaven's "lost and found" is different. Jesus claims the whole thing! No wonder the cartoon angel is smiling. With all the celebrating, it must be a great place to work.

Dear Jesus, there are times that I still feel lost, even though I am found. Give me assurance and peace. Amen.

Angels in the Far-Outfield

"In my Father's house there are many dwelling places. If it were not so, would I have told you that I go to prepare a place for you?"
—John 14:2

Even as you read this, Jesus is preparing a place for you in heaven. That beats even a beach house on the French Riviera any day of the week!

Your neighbors in that heavenly-place-to-come might not be ones you would choose. In fact, you might be surprised by who's there. All the more reason to learn to get along with the neighbors you have right now.

God of heaven, it's good to know there is a place for me—and for my neighbors near and far away—with you. Amen.

Got Any Souls? Go Fish.

And he said to them, "Follow me, and I will make you fish for people."
Immediately they left their nets and followed him.
—Matthew 4:19-20

The next time you're doing homework or chores, imagine a strange but radiant man walking up and talking to you about changing jobs. If you dropped everything to go with him, it probably would be a shock to your family (and maybe to you). However, that's what Jesus' disciples did when he said, "Follow me."

You might not be into baiting hooks and fishing, but Jesus says to you, "Follow me." Drop everything that keeps you from following. There's no luck involved in this fishing expedition. You'll have all that you need.

Jesus, who fished me from sin, you caught me! I'm happy to be in your net. But what amazes me is how you allow me to plumb the depths of love and possibility. Thank you. Amen.

My God Can Beat Up Your God

Amazing Feet of Love

Then he poured water into a basin and began to wash the disciples'
feet and to wipe them with the towel that was tied around him.
—John 13:5

Words can be contradicted, counter-argued, and debated to
death. Instead of words, Christ gives us the model for perfect
humility, service, and startling love when he insists on washing
his disciples' feet. Think about it: God incarnate stoops to scrub
dirty, crusty, stinky feet. What king or political leader could you
imagine doing such a thing? Come to think of it: How many of
the rest of us would dare repeat Christ's revolutionary act?

Loving, humble action—who can argue with that?

*God, cleanse my heart, then show me ways I may mirror the act
of washing feet—especially where my enemies and those I disagree
with are concerned. Amen.*

Martin Luther:
International Man of Mystery

"The one who believes in me will also do the works that I do and, in fact, will do greater works than these, because I am going to the Father."
—John 14:12

Martin Luther fought to correct a distorted view of God and faith. His namesake, Martin Luther King Jr., launched a civil rights revolution in America. Both of these men had opponents who tried to stop them and their radical ideas, but the movements they started continue on even today.

When Martin Luther and Martin Luther King Jr. saw what was going wrong in the church and society, they worked to bring change. With Christ at work in us, we can do the same.

I wonder what work you yearn to do through me, Jesus. I wonder how I will handle my enemies and opponents. Walk with me, because I can do all things through you. Amen.

What Feeds Your Faith?

The tempter came and said to him, "If you are the Son of God,
command these stones to become loaves of bread."
—Matthew 4:3

How long do you follow your New Year's resolutions? Or maybe
you don't make any resolutions so you won't have to worry about
breaking them!

When our lives get crazy-busy or just plain hard, we crack. Our
resolutions and good intentions get shaky. Maybe we keep on
doing something we know is wrong. Our faith might feel wobbly,
too. Once we cave in, what's left?

Well, actually, a lot. Jesus, who knows what it's like to be
tempted, is there for us even in the toughest of times, with
forgiveness, strength, and a new start.

*I need you, God of second chances. See through to my deepest
needs. Give me strength in times of weakness. Amen.*

The Scent of Dissent

And whatever you do, in word or deed, do everything in the name of
the Lord Jesus, giving thanks to God the Father through him.
—Colossians 3:17

Faced with persecution and the threat of death, we might beg for
a glass of water too. How many people would manage instead to
pour out words of hope and thanks to God?

The words in the Bible passage sound like the words of a happy
Christian in the most ideal of circumstances. But they aren't. Paul,
the writer, is stuck in prison for his beliefs. He has every reason
to grumble about the lousy food, mistreatment, and non-existent
sentencing guidelines. But what is he saying instead? "Give
thanks to God in everything."

*Lord of hope, I pray for an attitude of gratitude in all times. You
have blessed me beyond anything I could imagine. Let me start by
thanking you now. Amen.*

If Looks Could Kill

"And do not bring us to the time of trial,
but rescue us from the evil one."
—Matthew 6:13

Why did Jesus even mention *evil* when he taught his followers to pray? We know that bad, even evil, things happen to all kinds of people in all kinds of places. But we don't want to think about this any more than we have to, especially in a prayer.

Jesus lived on this earth. He knew evil is real. Maybe we don't need to be reminded of that. But we do need a reminder that God is our deliverer. God is working in our lives and gives us hope in the face of evil.

God who faces down evil, lead me and guide me. Fill me with hope in the face of evil. Amen.

A Kingdom Not of This World

"Do not be afraid, little flock, for it is your Father's
good pleasure to give you the kingdom."
—Luke 12:32

Heaven—a gated community with twenty-four-hour security and a
short list of people who can be allowed on the premises?

Well, no . . . and we can thank God for that!

In God's eternal kingdom, there are no gates or "No Trespassing"
signs. There's no security officer keeping people out or letting
them in. There's just Jesus, gathering people in left and right,
never even taking time for a break.

What a way to run the place!

God, bring in your kingdom, now and for all time. Amen.

You're Evil: May I See Your I.D.?

I do not do the good I want, but the evil I do not want is what I do.
—Romans 7:19

Even Paul, the great leader and teacher, struggled with sin and evil. Sometimes he even knew what was right and wanted to do it—and still did what was wrong.

We know what Paul is talking about, don't we? And to make things more complicated, sometimes evil is hidden or it looks . . . not so bad, really. That's when an evil detector would really come in handy, right?

Well, not so fast. Maybe there's something better out there. God has the power not only to detect evil, but to deliver us when we're in the middle of it.

That makes an evil detector as obsolete as a cassette tape.

God, thank you for rescuing me from sin and evil. Amen.

There's God Talk, and There's God's Talk

"Blessed are the pure in heart, for they will see God. Blessed are the peacemakers, for they will be called children of God."
—Matthew 5:8-9

We can try to win every argument about God, faith, and the church, but this is an uphill battle—especially if we think we're better than the people we're arguing with.

Instead, Jesus calls us to be peacemakers—striving to understand, build bridges, and look for ways to tackle heartbreaking problems from AIDS in Africa to poverty to homelessness to child abuse to domestic violence to loneliness and despair.

No argument there.

God, sometimes I'd rather argue about you. Help me to bring peace and build bridges instead. Amen.

Will Miracles Ever Cease?

And God is able to provide you with every blessing in abundance,
so that by always having enough of everything,
you may share abundantly in every good work.
—2 Corinthians 9:8

It's easy to believe the age of miracles is in the past. But even though we may not be pelted with manna, God does send a downpour of blessings to us.

These abundant blessings aren't meant to stop with us. What God gives freely to us—time, talents, money, bread, etc.—we are called to pass on to others. We share abundantly because God first shared abundantly with us.

God of abundance, help me to neither hide from nor hoard my blessings, but share them freely with others. Amen.

Stuff People Are Always Getting Wrong about God

Fee-Fi-Fo-Fum

God so loved the world . . .
—John 3:16

We blame God for everything from tornadoes to tragic deaths.
Many people view God as the giant from Jack and the Beanstalk:
"Fee-Fi-Fo-Fum, I smell the blood of an Englishman! Be he alive,
or be he dead, I'll have his bones to grind my bread." That would
make some gruesome toast.

Christ's death is shocking, but it's exactly the opposite of an
angry God who kills everyone who gets in the way. It's more
like an old war movie where one soldier throws himself onto a
grenade, allowing the rest of the platoon to live. It's because of
love and care for you that Christ gave his life. Better yet, he didn't
stay dead. Christ rose again. You will too.

*God of love, I'm sorry for blaming you for things that aren't your
fault. Help me see the ways that you care for me. Amen.*

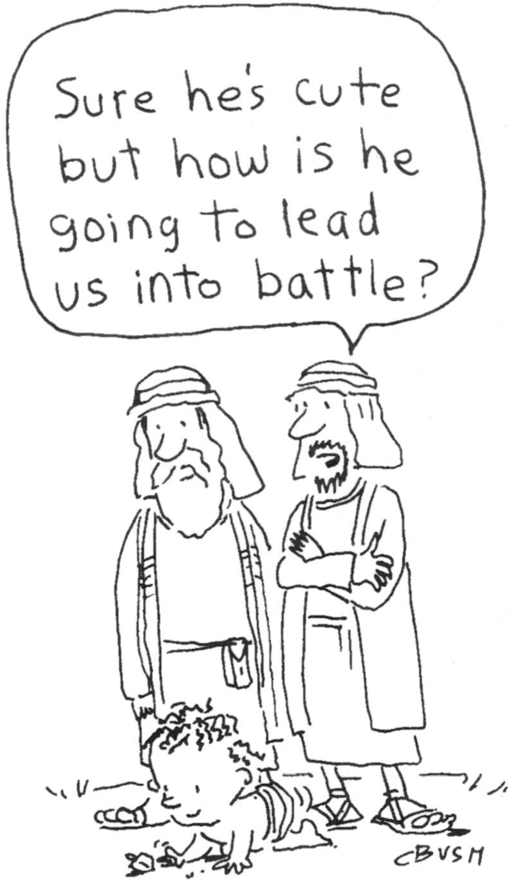
Sure he's cute but how is he going to lead us into battle?
CBUSM

You Can't Say
"Coochy-Coochy-Coo" to a General

Once He was small, when He lay in the manger; and yet even then
He was so great that He was worshiped by angels . . .
—Martin Luther

It's probably not a good idea to play "Peek-a-Boo" with a four-star general. But there was a day when you could play "This Little Piggy Went to Market" with the Son of God. Jesus Christ kept everyone guessing. When people wanted a prince, he was born in a barn. When people wanted a warrior, he was a servant. When people wanted him to knock heads together, he suffered and died on the cross. When people thought he was dead, he rose again.

There's one thing you can know for sure; Jesus gives you his goodness and now you're a child too . . . a child of God.

Jesus, you surprise me. Thanks for being so much more than I could ever imagine. Amen.

You Say, "Tomato"; I Say, "Pomodoro"

"... say to the Israelites, 'I AM has sent me to you.'"
—Exodus 3:14

Find yourself a Christian Sunday school in Saudi Arabia and the little kids will be singing about Allah.

"Wait a second," you ask, "isn't Allah the name of the Muslim God?"

Yes, it is. Muslims, Jews, and Christians all trace their roots back to the God of Creation, the God of Abraham and Sarah.

"Hold on," you exclaim, "what's going on here?"

Allah is Arabic for God. When Arabic-speaking Christians say "Allah," they mean "Father, Son, and Holy Spirit."

There are many names for God in the Bible. Watch for them. Sing them. Use them to talk to God in prayer.

No single name is big enough to describe you, God. Thanks for being so complex. Amen.

Bible People

All scripture is inspired by God.
—2 Timothy 3:16

What if the Bible were written like *People* magazine? Here are some possible headlines:

Adam and Eve Start a Nudist Colony
Baby's Father Is 100 Years Old
How Mary Lost That Pesky Baby Weight

The Bible and *People* magazine are similar in that they contain stories about real people (and some of those stories are scandalous). The similarities stop there.

People is about people. The Bible is about God loving people.

People contains fashion advice. The Bible contains the saga of God's love for us.

The Bible is more than a collection of stories. It reveals God's love. Its pages don't carry juicy gossip—they carry Christ.

Thanks for giving us more than advice in the Bible, God. Thanks for giving us Jesus. Amen.

Put Some God In Your Tank!

To discuss it briefly, misuse of the divine name occurs most obviously
in worldly business and in matters involving money, property,
and honor, whether publicly in court or in the market . . .
—Martin Luther

It's not hard to spot an improper use of God's name. We can find
plenty of examples in the media. Come to think of it, maybe we
don't need to look any further than ourselves.

It's harder to spot a proper use of God's name. For this, we need
to look at places where people are praising, thanking, teaching,
serving, and praying in God's name.

*I'm so glad to be on a first-name basis with you, God. Thanks for
introducing yourself to me. Amen.*

It's for Your Own Good

... fools despise wisdom and instruction.
—Proverbs 1:7b

Dear God,

My kids say I'm ruining their lives. They cannot watch TV until their homework is done and they must be home by 7:00 on weeknights.

Sincerely,

Am I Mean?

Dear Am I Mean?,

I hear you. A parent's job is to keep kids safe and healthy. But kids don't like rules, even the ones that are good for them. So sometimes they think we're mean or trying to take away all their fun.

Do what I do. Keep on loving your children, no matter what.

Dear God, I thank you for parents and rules (if I have to). Amen.

Opinions Shared in This Devotional Do Not Reflect the Views of Your Favorite Infomercial

---

... we should not despise (God's) Word and the preaching of the same, but deem it holy and gladly hear and learn it.
—Martin Luther

Some ways to encourage people to go to worship:

- Tell them to go.
- Go by yourself.
- Invite them to go with you.

In worship we enter into the presence of the Living God who made heaven and earth and also desires to bless us with all that is good, including the real presence of Jesus Christ himself.

This is meant to be shared. Invite someone to go to worship with you today.

Living God, I can be with you and your people in worship. Thank you. Amen.

Ho-Hum

Keep straight the path of your feet, and all your ways will be sure.
—Proverbs 4:26

Exciting stuff in the Bible:

- Two thousand demons possess a scary naked guy.
- A huge fish swallows, saves, and pukes up Jonah.
- Jesus defeats death itself.

Not-so-exciting stuff in the Bible:

- How to treat your parents.
- What to do with meat that's been sacrificed to idols.
- How to talk about your friends when they're not around.

The not-so-exciting stuff in the Bible is usually law—giving rules about what to do and what not to do. This stuff is important, but it's not all we have. The exciting stuff—the gospel—tells about Christ's love, forgiveness, and holiness for us. That's nothing to yawn at.

Dear God, I know the rules are important, and I really like the parts with Jesus. Thank you for both. Amen.

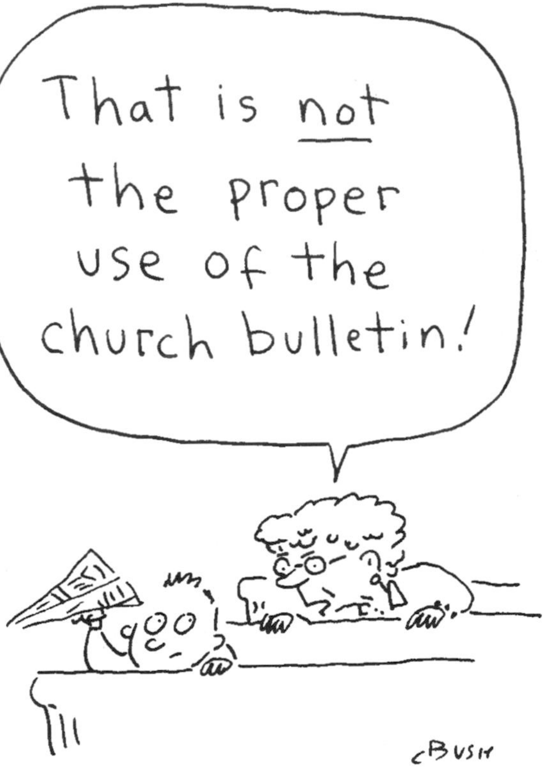
That is not the proper use of the church bulletin!
Bush

Let the Little Children Be Seen and Not Heard?

For everything there is a season.
—Ecclesiastes 3:1

Which bothers God more: the little boy playing with his bulletin or the lady frowning and crabbing at him? Some folks think that "Don't run in God's house" and "Sit still" should be carved in stone at the tail end of the Commandments.

We wouldn't do well to simply ignore those who desire silence in, and the absence of footprints on the ceiling of, the sanctuary. But then, we wouldn't do well to ignore Jesus, who scolded the scolders and then lifted some runny-nosed kids to his knee, saying that they were the standard for true faith.

Sometimes worship means being silent. But don't forget, we are worshiping the God who created the duck-billed platypus. Sometimes worship means having silly fun.

Lord of the duck-billed platypus, thank you for thinking up the idea of fun. Amen.

Checking It Twice

"I will remember their sins no more."
—Hebrews 8:12

Some people picture God keeping a long list of all our blunders—and checking it twice like some crabby Santa. But instead of toys, people think God is dishing out punishment.

Throw that idea out the window. In the case of forgiven sins, God is forgetful.

We're the ones with the long memory. We can use our memory against those who have wronged us, which isn't actually forgiveness. Or we can forgive those who have wronged us and use our memory to protect ourselves.

Forgiving does not mean forgetting or allowing someone to harm us. It means telling the truth about what someone did and loving them anyway. And it takes God's power to do that. That's what forgiven people do . . . they forgive.

Hey, God, remember that sin I confessed a while back? You don't? Thanks. Amen.

Do Guardian Angels Protect Speeders?

One should acknowledge civil laws, submit to them,
and respect their authority.
—Martin Luther

Francine knew she was busted. She considered her options:

- Holler at the police officer for stopping her when she was only going 38 miles per hour over the speed limit.

- Cry.

- Confess.

- Claim the devil made her do it.

- Deny that she was even driving the car.

- Confess and then insist that the police officer is anti-Christian if he doesn't forgive her.

- Jump out of the car and run for it.

God's forgiveness covers our sins, but it doesn't give us permission to break civil laws. God will forgive Francine, even if she gets a ticket. But the police officer doesn't have to.

Forgiving God, thank you for loving me, even when I (place verb here). Amen.

To Land as Promised

[Jesus] said to him, "You shall love the Lord your God with all your heart, and with all your soul, and with all your mind. This is the greatest and first commandment. And a second is like it: 'You shall love your neighbor as yourself.'"
—Matthew 22:37-39

"Love God with all of your heart, soul, and strength." How do we do this? Because the answer is not clear-cut, we pray to and confide in God—and develop a relationship that brings us closer to the mystery than, say, any road map.

And "love your neighbor?" This includes people in far-off places, but it begins in the very places we live, play, and work each day.

Commanding, compassionate Lord, I want to stop treating my life as a series of hoops to jump through. Your kingdom, though an adventure, is not an amusement park. It is a place where I am challenged to become the person you created me to be. Help and lead me. Amen.

The Problem with God's Love (Is That It's Also for People You Might Not Like So Much)

You Can't Judge a Book by Its Cover, But You Can Judge a Book by Its Savior

. . . all of you are one in Christ Jesus.
—Galatians 3:28

Here's an idea. To make it easy to tell who's a Christian (and who's not), we could all dress like Jesus. Get in line for your sandals and robe! Okay? Well . . . maybe not.

Hairstyle and wardrobe choices might identify us as part of one culture or another, but they don't identify our faith. Wearing a suit doesn't make someone any more Christian than wearing a Mohawk.

You might be baffled by the stuffed shirts sitting in the pew in front of you, but they have been marked by the same cross as you have. The radical love of Jesus is exactly the same for each of us—that's what makes us one and the same.

Lord of all, help me see people the way you see them. Amen.

I was going to bite You, but then I realized that You are one of God's creatures too.
BUSH

Jesus Is Not Fair

Therefore, take your enemies and the ungrateful and do good to them.
—Martin Luther

The way the world looks at things, no one would blame you for seeking revenge against the school bully who hung your pants from the flagpole.

The problem is, the same Jesus who died and rose again for you died and rose again for your archenemy. And this is just plain unfair by the world's standards.

That's the thing about God's grace. No one deserves it, yet it's given for all. It's the same unfair grace that Jesus used when he forgave the guys nailing him to the cross—while they were swinging the hammers.

It's unfair, but it's not so bad—because each day we need that sort of grace too.

God of undeserved grace, thank you for giving me what I need, not what I deserve. Help me to treat others differently because of the way you have treated me. Amen.

One

Such unity is not possible outside of the realm of faith.
—Martin Luther

Some people say the world has more than 30,000 different groups of Christians. (Quick, name 100 if you can.)

With that many different Christian groups, for sure there will be differences among us. Our problem is that we let our differences become reasons to label others as "not really Christian."

Some congregations are big; some small. Some use guitars; some use no music at all. Some are strict; some not so strict. Some do stuff in worship that would make you cringe. Yet we are all one Christian church. That's what we mean when we say we believe in the "holy catholic church" in the Apostles' Creed. We are one not because we are similar; we are one because we all belong to Jesus.

Making all of us Christians into one must be tough, God. I praise you for your miracles. Amen.

Let's Be Friends

"Just as you did it to one of the least of these
who are members of my family, you did it to me."
—Matthew 25:40

People You'd Rather Not Care about:

- Guy who always wants to show you his scabs.

- Girl who calls her pencils by name.

- Guy who belches love songs to you.

- Girl who told everybody your locker combination.

People Jesus Cares about and Calls You to Care about:

- Guy who always wants to show you his scabs.

- Girl who calls her pencils by name.

- Guy who belches love songs to you.

- Girl who told everybody your locker combination.

*There are plenty of people I'd really rather not care about, Lord.
But I know you love them. Help me to love them too. Amen.*

The Lord Be With You, Slimeball.
Also With You, Jerk.

The peace of God, which surpasses all understanding,
will guard your hearts and your minds in Christ Jesus.
—Philippians 4:7

What happens when we are left on our own to care about each other? The mood never comes.

The thing is, our peace is fickle. If it's our peace we're supposed to dish out, we've got long lists of people who we think shouldn't share in our peace.

But it's the peace of God that we share at worship. And there's plenty of that to go around. God's peace works. It heals you and the person you share it with.

Send your peace to me, Lord, and help me to share it freely with others. Amen.

Not My Fault

There is no longer Jew or Greek, there is no longer slave or free, there is no longer male and female; for all of you are one in Christ Jesus.
—Galatians 3:28

North vs. South

Men vs. Women

Jocks vs. Geeks

Republicans vs. Democrats

If there are 6 billion people in the world then there must be 5,999,999,999 ways we separate ourselves from each other. It all started in the Garden of Eden. When God asked Adam if he ate the forbidden fruit, Adam blamed it on Eve, who blamed it on the serpent.

Ever since then, we've become masters at feeling better about ourselves by pointing out the faults of those around us. We've all got faults. Jesus is the only perfect one. But instead of separating his perfect self from us, he *gives* his perfect self to us.

Dear Jesus, thank you for taking us all into your open arms. Amen.

Jesus Loves the Little Weasels

[Jesus] looked up and said to him, "Zacchaeus, hurry and come down;
for I must stay at your house today." So he hurried down and was
happy to welcome him. All who saw it began to grumble and said,
"He has gone to be the guest of one who is a sinner."
—Luke 19:5-7

Of all people to hang out with, Jesus picked Zacchaeus, someone
who collected taxes from his own people for the occupying army,
cheating and demanding even more than what was required all
the while.

Zacchaeus wasn't the sort of person who would win a popularity
contest, but God cared about him anyway. And it takes that sort
of God to love someone like you. Think about it.

*Lord, there are some people who really make my blood boil. Help
me to see that you gave your blood for them, like you gave it for
me. Amen.*

Get Off My Yard

"Which of these three, do you think, was a neighbor to the man who fell into the hands of the robbers?" He said, "The one who showed him mercy." Jesus said to him, "Go and do likewise."
—Luke 10:36-37

Good Neighbors

- Bring chocolate chip cookies to your door.
- Don't care if your band practices until 1 A.M.
- Babysit your goldfish when you're on vacation.
- Loan you a cup of sugar.

Bad Neighbors

- Bring complaints to your door.
- Practice the accordion until 2 A.M.
- Send their dogs to your yard to avoid clean-up duty.
- "Borrow" your cable TV connection.

Your Neighbors

- Include "good" neighbors and "bad" neighbors from all over the planet.

Show me my neighbors, Jesus. Give me your love for them. Amen.

Words That You Probably Have Not Used in the Last Week

Do You Know what adultery means?
Not acting like a kidery?
BUSH

It's Not Just for Married People Anymore

"We should fear and love God, and so we should lead
a chaste and pure life in word and deed . . ."
—Martin Luther

Most people think adultery means husbands and wives cheating on each other. That's right, but it's not the whole story. The command against adultery kicks in way before people walk down the aisle:

- When an ad uses sex to sell toothpaste (or anything).
- When we tell or laugh at a nasty joke about sex.
- When we want someone for ourselves, just because he or she is with someone else.

It isn't "kid stuff" to have our words and actions show that sex is the special gift from God that it is.

Thanks for making us male and female, Lord. That was a pretty good idea. Help me with the purity and decency part, because that can get tough sometimes. Amen.

Nice Bike, Hand It Over

"We know how to put up a fine front to conceal our rascality."
—Martin Luther

The Commandments list stealing before coveting, but in our lives *coveting* always comes first. Coveting means wanting something so bad that you begin to think you deserve it and you plan a way to "acquire" it.

These equations demonstrate the idea:

Bill likes Andre's favorite video game + (Bill borrows video game + Bill always *forgets* to return video game) = Bill now possesses video game. Therefore: Bill liked, then coveted, then stole the game.

(Leann + Sally + Veronica = Best Friends) x Leann tells nasty lies about Sally to Veronica = Sally gets left out of the friendship. Therefore: Leann coveted Veronica's friendship and stole it from Sally.

God of all good gifts, please convince me to be satisfied with what and who you have given me. Thanks. Amen.

Home Is Where the Faith Is

If I take the wings of the morning
and settle at the farthest limits of the sea,
even there your hand shall lead me,
and your right hand shall hold me fast.
—Psalm 139:9-10

To be in exile means to be banished from your home and country against your will. Away from your own stuff. Away from everything that makes you feel safe and secure. That would stink.

Odds are that you are not currently being driven from your home or country. But exile comes in other ways too. Sometimes we feel alone and abandoned, even when we're surrounded by people.

But we have "*inxile*," too. (You won't find *inxile* in the dictionary. It's a made-up word that means the opposite of exile.) In the midst of any exile—physical, emotional, relational—we have the promise that Jesus Christ is with us.

Wherever you are (no matter how much it stinks), God is there.

Lord, thanks for being here. Amen.

Pointing the Finger

Thus says the Lord God of hosts . . .
—Isaiah 22:15

Prophets speak for God:

- The prophet Hosea marries a hooker to show how the people were cheating on God. He also demonstrates how God wins us back.
- The prophet Ezekiel eats a scroll so he can preach God's word to the people.
- The prophet Nathan exposes King David as a rapist and murderer and points him to forgiveness.

People in power often fear and hate them, but prophets speak the truth anyway. Even though God's truth might hurt at first, it always sets us free.

God of the prophets, when you point out the hard truth about me, please give me Jesus too—the Truth that sets me free. Amen.

Busy Prepositions

"Let my people go."
—Exodus 5:1

Prepositions (words like "of," "in," "from," and "through") connect nouns, pronouns, and phrases to other words in a sentence. We need a lot of prepositions to talk about the Exodus:

God saved the people *of* Israel *from* slavery; led them *out of* Egypt, *through* the Red Sea and *into* the Promised Land.

It was tough going and the people of Israel complained a lot, but they were never alone. God was always *with* them, always leading them. They had to trust God, and God always provided for them.

We are connected to God too. By baptism into Christ, we get our own set of prepositions:

We become children *of* God saved *from* sin and look forward *to* the resurrection. It will be tough sometimes, but God is always *with* us.

Thanks for being in, with, under, above, before, *and* after *me, God. Amen.*

There's a Strong Family Resemblance

"I will make of you a great nation, and I will bless you, and make your name great, so that you will be a blessing."
—Genesis 12:2

As a matter of basic biology, *begetting* is passing on DNA and lineage. In other words, it's the way you have your dad's nose, your mom's earlobes, and your grandparents' German (or Kenyan or Swiss or Polynesian) last name.

As a matter of faith, *begetting* is the passing on of spiritual DNA. Way back in the book of Genesis, God gave Sarah and Abraham a promise—not only would they be blessed, they would be a blessing to the whole world. God was with them through thick and thin, no matter what dangers or frustrations they faced.

Through baptism into Jesus we become part of this promise. God is with us, blesses us, and sends us to bless the world.

God of Sarah and Abraham, thank you for your blessings. Make me a blessing too. Amen.

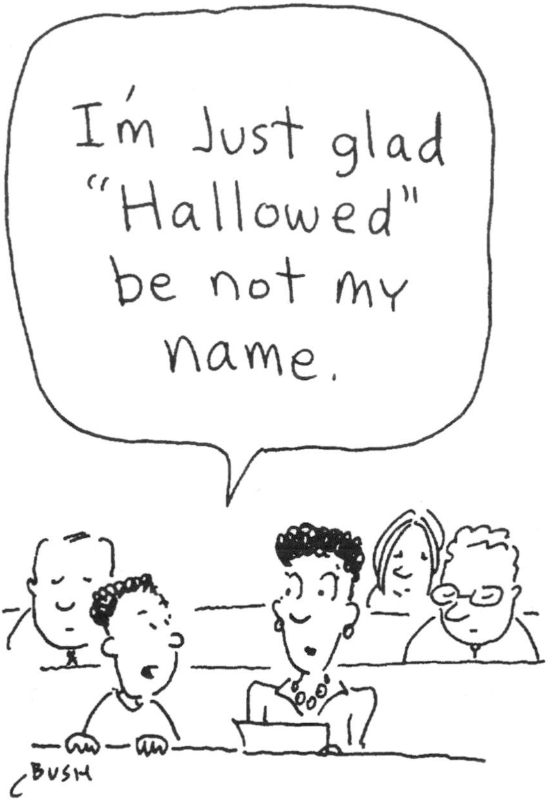
I'm Just glad "Hallowed" be not my name.
BUSH

Would You Rather Be Called Balthazar?

But you are a chosen race, a royal priesthood,
a holy nation, God's own people.
—1 Peter 2:9

Hallowed means holy, set apart for a special purpose. God's name is holy for us when we worship and live as if God really matters in our lives.

Although his mom will never say, "Hallowed Smith, come and wash your hands before supper," the cartoon boy's name is holy because Christ has claimed him.

When Christ calls you by name, you become someone new. You are set apart for God's plan in this world. And that's why God really matters in your life.

Thank you, God, for calling me by name, claiming me, and making me new. Amen.

Better Than Cake

He who saved the three men in the furnace
of the Babylonian king still lives and rules.
—Martin Luther

Salivation is when you drool over chocolate cake. It comes from glands in your mouth and helps you digest food. *Salvation* is when Jesus rescues you from sin, death, and the devil. It comes from Christ and gives you hope for this life and the next.

Three extraordinary acts of salivation:

- Getting locked overnight in a candy store.
- Walking past that cinnamon bun store in the mall.
- Your dog watching you eat steak.

Three extraordinary acts of salvation:

- God parting the Red Sea.
- A big fish swallowing Jonah, then puking him up.
- Jesus dying on the cross and rising to life again.

Thanks, God, for (list your three favorite foods). Thanks even more for Jesus. Amen.

Your Attention for Annunciations, Please

... the angel Gabriel was sent by God ...
—Luke 1:26

An *annunciation* is an announcement, but not just any announcement. It's way more important than hearing that today's school lunch is tacos or that the biology class won't be dissecting today because someone liberated the frogs.

The most important annunciation in the Bible came when the angel Gabriel told a normal teenager named Mary that a baby would be born who would save the world and, by the way, the baby would be God's Son; and, also by the way, she would be the mom.

That annunciation is still repeated by little angels to little girls in blue bathrobes in Christmas pageants all around the world. It's just as great today as it was the first time.

Keep the good news coming, God. I don't ever get tired of hearing it. Amen.

I Wanna Go Home

Do not despair; God has had regard for you.
—Martin Luther

Eczema—an inflammation that causes extremely itchy, dry, red patches on the skin.

Diaspora—any people or population forced to leave their homeland.

Diaspora sounds like a skin rash, but it's worse.

Being chased out of their own country was a terrible thing for the people of Israel, but they discovered something terribly important. They had to leave behind everything they owned, but they still had God. Better yet, God still had them.

When you question where God is in your life, remember this: no matter how terrible it is, Christ is there with you in every place and situation.

Sometimes my faith gets itchy, Lord. Please clear it up and hold me when I am scared. Amen.

Worms Have 0.7 Calories

"Here I stand."
—Martin Luther

If the Diet of Worms was a fad food diet, would you sign up?

No one would get very strong on a diet of worms, but at the Diet of Worms Martin Luther showed that God's love and grace gave him all the strength he needed.

For sixteenth-century monks like Luther, a diet had nothing to do with food. It was a trial, so if you were "on a diet," you were in trouble. Worms was the German city where Luther was put "on a diet" for rocking the boat.

People at the trial tried to get Luther to take back stuff he had said about God's love and grace, but it would have been easier for Luther to eat worms. Instead he said, "Here I stand."

Gracious God, thanks for giving me—and Luther—a place to stand. Amen.

These Little Piggies Went Swimming

"Come out of the man, you unclean spirit!"
—Mark 5:8

Exercising is moving your muscles. It's good for you.

Exorcising is booting demons out of people. Good for people, bad for demons.

There was a man who was so tormented that he lived among tombs, far from any people.

Jesus didn't have to stop for this man, but he did. He exorcised the man's demons and sent them on their way into a herd of pigs. The pigs, and the demons in them, ended up drowning in a sea.

People who saw what happened were afraid. That's not the end of the story, however. The man started telling what Jesus had done, and everyone who heard him was amazed.

Lord, please liberate me from things that torment me. Amen.

I can deal with loss and grief. I Just couldn't stand the loss of grief.

Good Grief!

"Blessed are those who mourn, for they will be comforted."
—Matthew 5:4

Some losses are hard to swallow. Some we can't prepare for. And anyone who has lost knows words of hollow "chin up" comfort at best lack empathy, and at worst sound insensitive.

That brings us to the essence of what it means to be comforted. We walk with those who mourn, just as we hope others will walk with us. God walks with us too—a welcome presence in our hour of need.

With grief, mourning gives way, at last, to morning—a new day when loss is transformed into the fabric of an ongoing life.

Wonderful Counselor, Beautiful Consoler, the thought of grief and loss makes me sad. I would rather think about blessings and joys. Help me to see grief as a way of honoring life. Amen.

Attitude Adjustment

Attitude Is a Choice

[God's] steadfast love endures forever.
—Psalm 136:1

When you face tough times in your life, you have a choice: How will you respond? Will you get grumpy and angry? Pout and snap at your family? What will your attitude be?

It's never easy to deal with problems and stresses in our lives. But God promises to always love us. Psalm 136 describes God's "steadfast" love. God loves us with love that lasts, and doesn't drop us just because we are sad or mad or scared.

When something bad happens to you, you can either gripe or cope. Hard times can make us sad or angry, but not permanently. We can turn our attitude around by remembering God's steadfast love.

God, give me an attitude adjustment when I am angry about unimportant things. Thanks for loving me always. Amen.

God Loves Me More than You!

My people are bent on turning away from me.
—Hosea 11:7

The books of 1 and 2 Kings tell about the division of the Israelite kingdom. First, Israel was ruled by one king. Then, after a bitter struggle, the kingdom was divided into two: Israel and Judah. Both kingdoms kept turning away from the Lord.

We have a tendency to argue about minor concerns. We fight over rivalries that aren't important. In one way or another, we have all been "bent on turning away" from God. In Hosea 11, God is sad because the people continue to turn away from God's love and compassion. What does God want from us? God hopes we will give God our hearts, instead of turning against each other and away from God.

I'm sorry that I get involved in petty arguments, God. Forgive me. Amen.

God's Way or Pharaoh's Way?

For my thoughts are not your thoughts,
nor are your ways my ways, says the Lord.
—Isaiah 55:8

Pharaoh rules by dominating people. Pharaoh enslaved the Hebrew people, using them as cheap labor to accomplish his grand plans.

God saw the Hebrew people in slavery and carried out a plan to free them. Through a serious of plagues, God tried to convince Pharaoh to have a change of heart. Pharaoh's heart may not have changed, but the plagues did eventually change his actions.

There are forces in our lives that work like Pharaoh: people who want to use us or hurt us. But God still rules with love and compassion, and works to free us from anyone and anything that causes pain and enslavement.

God, your ways are better than our ways. Thank you for showing us love and compassion. Amen.

That's Not What the Bible Says

"You have heard that it was said, 'An eye for an eye and a tooth
for a tooth.' But I say to you, Do not resist an evildoer. But if
anyone strikes you on the right cheek, turn the other also."
—Matthew 5:38-39

Long ago, common people didn't read the Bible. Priests told
them what the Latin Bible meant. After Martin Luther translated
the Bible into German, regular people could read Scripture for
themselves.

Today we have Bibles in more translations than we can count. All
the translations have different purposes and different styles, but
all are the Bible. Although it can be scary to try to read such an
important and sacred book and figure out what it's saying, we can
learn a lot about ourselves and about God by doing this.

*God, I trust that the Bible is your holy Word. Help me to read and
understand it for myself. Amen.*

Jesus the Rebel

When the chief priests and the Pharisees heard his parables,
they realized that he was speaking about them. They wanted
to arrest him, but they feared the crowds.
—Matthew 21:45-46

If you grew up hearing Jesus' story, you may not think his message is that radical. But the truth is, Jesus made some people mad. He questioned and confronted people in authority. He broke religious rules: he healed on the Sabbath, he touched lepers, and he ate with tax collectors and other "sinners." He made many enemies when he taught about the Son of Man and the Messiah.

Despite all this, many people did sign on to Jesus' teachings. And, ironically, Jesus did die and come to life again. Many people since then have called him their Savior and King.

God, help me to understand Jesus' radical message and be bold in my faith life. Amen.

Who Cares?

Jesus went on with his disciples to the villages of Caesarea Philippi;
and on the way he asked his disciples, "Who do people say that I am?"
—Mark 8:27

Maybe Jesus was wondering about his reputation when he asked this question: "What do people think of me?"

Sometimes we worry about our reputations. What will our friends think if we go to youth group? What will popular people at school say if we wear Christian T-shirts? What will the kids in the cafeteria say if we pray before lunch? Maybe we don't usually care that much about what these people think, but we get embarrassed about our faith choices.

Jesus is the Messiah, the one who comes to save us. What you think and say about him is far more important than what people think and say about you.

God, I know who you are. Thank you for loving me for who I am. Amen.

What Do You Believe?

If you confess with your lips that Jesus is Lord and believe in your heart that God raised him from the dead, you will be saved.
—Romans 10:9

How do we deal with friends who are not Christian? Are we the only people with the truth?

After reading the Bible passage above we might ask, "So what happens if we *don't* confess with our lips and believe in our hearts? What then? Are we going to hell?" The Scriptures say that some choices draw people closer to God and others move them away from God. The Bible indicates that belief does matter. But above all, the Bible shows us that our God is a God of grace.

Let's live what we believe—and leave the heaven-and-hell debate to God.

God, sometimes your word is confusing to me. Help my unbelief and let me trust you. Amen.

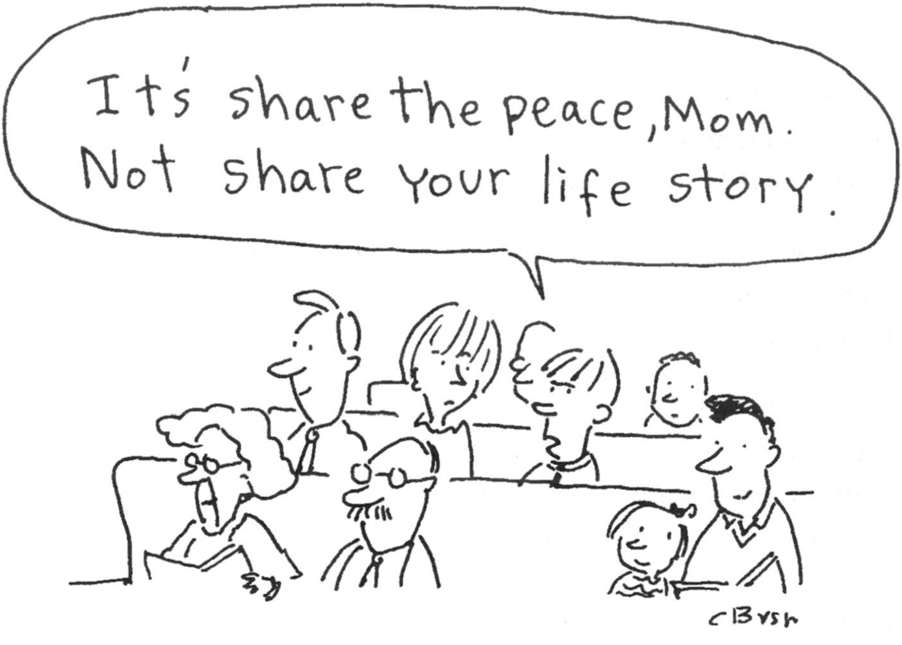
It's share the peace, Mom.
Not share your life story.

Too Much Information

So then, putting away falsehood, let all of us speak the truth
to our neighbors, for we are members of one another.
—Ephesians 4:25

Maybe you know someone who has TMI disease. No matter who they're talking to, they have to share their life story. They provide TOO MUCH INFORMATION (TMI) everywhere they go.

When we share the peace in church, we share the peace that comes from Christ. If we spend the whole time sharing with one person, we can't share with others.

If your parents have TMI, ask them to respect your privacy when they share. And if *you* have TMI, think about this: God already knows every detail of your life story. Then try sharing the peace with a few more people than you usually do.

God, you know my life story even if I don't say anything. Let me trust you with it. Amen.

On a Mission from God

"Go therefore and make disciples of all nations, baptizing them
in the name of the Father and of the Son and of the Holy Spirit,
and teaching them to obey everything that I have commanded you."
—Matthew 28:19-20

Sometimes being a disciple isn't all it's cracked up to be. It sounds so noble: Go into all the world, baptizing, teaching, and making new disciples. But sometimes the people don't like us. Sometimes they don't believe us. Sometimes they are downright hostile. Sometimes they call us names. Sometimes all we've got to show for days of hard mission work is blisters and sore muscles—or a lousy tunic.

Whether the results are fast or slow, whether our efforts are rewarded or not, God calls us to share the good news and bring the message of Jesus wherever we go.

God, help me to be a bold witness for you. Amen.

Manna, Again?

"If only we had meat to eat! We remember the fish we used to eat
in Egypt for nothing, the cucumbers, the melons, the leeks,
the onions, and the garlic; but now our strength is dried up,
and there is nothing at all but this manna to look at."
—Numbers 11:4-6

The Israelites came down with a bad case of tunnel vision while
they wandered in the wilderness. They fondly remembered how
well they ate in Egypt—in the days when they had plenty to eat—
but they forgot that they were slaves during that time! All they
could think about was the manna that appeared each day, the
only food available to eat.

The people would have starved while wandering in the wilderness,
but God provided the food they needed—just not the food they
wanted.

*God, thank you providing what I need, though not always what I
want. Amen.*

Things You Might Not Have Known about God

Back to the Drawing Board

The sea is his, for he made it, and the dry land,
which his hands have formed.
—Psalm 95:5

God put some thought into making the world. Who knows, maybe there were some ideas that God came up with, got excited about, and then said, "Nah! That'll never work."

Look around our world. It was all God's idea. God had fun with creation. Duck-billed platypus? God's idea. Giraffe? God's idea. Mt. Everest? Yep, God's idea. The sound that rain makes? That's God's idea too.

And from the highest mountain to the most colorful tropical fish, you are the pinnacle of everything God made.

Creator God, thank you for coming up with the idea of (strange animal) and thank you for giving us (your favorite color). Those were great ideas and only you could come up with them! Thanks for making me too. Amen.

Angels Are Real

The good news was preached and sung for us by angels.
—Martin Luther

Angels:

- sometimes have wings.
- deliver messages from God.
- inspire awe in people.
- are holy.

You:

- never have wings.
- deliver messages from God.
- inspire awe in your grandparents, yet annoy your parents.
- are holy.

In the Bible you will usually find angels singing songs about how awesome God is, or zipping around earth delivering messages from God to humans. We're called to praise God and deliver God's messages too.

Dear God, show me where I can bring your message today. Amen.

No, Really; It's Free

Lord, whatever [good] there is in us exists by thy grace.
—Martin Luther

God's grace is like mercury. It's potent, and any time you try to take hold of it for yourself it slips through your fingers.

Grace is powerful because it does what it says. Jesus uses his grace to claim you as a child of God and to forgive you, heal you, and give you a future.

Grace is so free that you can't even call and order a complimentary package of it from an infomercial. You can only hear it—so read the capitalized sentence out loud a few times. Better yet, read it to someone else, and then have them read it to you.

JESUS CHRIST DIED AND ROSE AGAIN TO MAKE YOU A CHILD OF GOD.

Dear Jesus, thank you. Just thank you. Amen.

God Has a Plan for You

I know the plans I have for you, says the LORD, plans for your welfare
and not for harm, to give you a future with hope.
—Jeremiah 29:11

The hard thing about God's plan for you is that it might not be real obvious. You aren't likely to get blueprints for your life the way Noah did.

The great thing about God's plan for you is that it might not be real obvious. The sky's the limit. You might not get a road map for God's plans, but Scripture and worship can point you in the right direction.

You can also take cues from your talents and stuff you love to do. You can bet God is steering you in the right direction.

Show me your way, Lord. Amen.

The Whole World's in God's Hands

Then I saw a new heaven and a new earth; for the first heaven
and the first earth had passed away, and the sea was no more.
—Revelation 21:1

The old Sunday school song says, "He's got the whole world in his
hands," and then makes a list. You and me, brother. You and me
sister. Little tiny baby.

Those are all true and good but what about the duck-billed
platypus and the ozone layer? They were both God's idea and
creation. And let's not forget the giraffe and the weeping willow
tree.

People have been pretty rough on this third rock from the sun.
Luckily, the God who is good to us sinners is good to the globe
too. God has promised a new heaven and new earth.

*I love your imagination, God. The colors, the plants, and the
animals are so good. Thanks for saving us humans. Please use me
to help in your fixing of the earth. Amen.*

God Wants to Hear from You

Moses says: "And the Lord granted his prayer," so the Lord will not disregard our sighs and cries either. Only let us be stirred up to pray.
—Martin Luther

Fifteen ways to pray:

1. Sing a Sunday school song.
2. Pray silently.
3. If you are angry, say so.
4. Draw a prayer.
5. Play a prayer on a musical instrument.
6. Adore God. (You're awesome, God!)
7. Confess.
8. Thank God.
9. Say a prayer for other people.
10. Cry.
11. Laugh.
12. Just listen.
13. Read some psalms.
14. Kneel at your bedside and talk to God.
15. Walk or run while you pray.

Sometimes I get tongue-tied, Holy Spirit. Thanks for your help in praying. Amen.

God Is Not Scared of the Dark

"Therefore I will not restrain my mouth;
I will speak in the anguish of my spirit;
I will complain in the bitterness of my soul."
—Job 7:11

Our "darkest hour" is the time when life seems scary or hopeless. It might be the death of a loved one or discovering that friends have been talking behind your back. Darkest hours involve pain that seems as if it will never go away and the feeling of being very alone.

Your darkest hour just might be the best time to act like a little kid. What do little kids do when they are lost and scared in the dark? They holler and cry, "Help me!"

The thing about crying out to God is that we discover that the One who is not scared of anything was right there with us the entire time.

Big brave God, please hold my hand when I'm scared. Amen.

God Wants Your Help

"You give them something to eat."
—Mark 6:37

Things God can do that we can't:

- Dream up and create the kiwi fruit.
- Keep the earth spinning on course.
- Raise the dead.
- Be omnipresent.
- Fulfill the Commandments.

Things God can do, but wants us to do anyway:

- Stick up for people who everyone else ignores.
- Teach Sunday school.
- Feed the hungry.
- Populate the planet.
- Forgive.

There is a reason you're good at—and love—organizing stuff. That's not your gift? Then there's a reason you've got such a wild imagination. That's not it? Well . . . whatever you really shine at, there's a reason.

God could have created a puppet stage and run everything alone, but that would have been boring. Instead, you've been created, gifted, and set free to share God's work in this world.

Let's roll, God. Amen.

The Creator Created You to Be Creative

Whatever the man called every living creature, that was its name.
—Genesis 2:19

Here is a portion of God's "to-do" list. Please select items that you can do with God.

- Keep track of expansion of universe.
- Rain.
- Create faith.
- Play a musical instrument.
- Draw.
- Train animals.
- Sing.
- Be all-powerful.
- Hear all prayers—and answer them.
- Pick up litter.
- Grow a garden.
- Send a rainbow over Canton, South Dakota.
- Make preparations for the resurrection.
- Forgive sins.
- Keep believers in true faith.
- Paint.
- Send snow to Sweden.
- Smile at a stranger.
- Love.
- Play a sport.
- Learn.

God, I like the odds of success when I work for you. Thanks for including me. Amen.

God Is Full of Surprises

Therefore earnestly pray to God that he may leave the Word with you,
for some surprising things are going to happen.
—Martin Luther

The book of Esther is full of surprises:

- God is never mentioned.

- Esther stumbles into becoming a hero.

- Bad guy Haman finds out that the joke is on him. He had tricked the king into setting a date to annihilate all the Jews in the land but, thanks to Esther's bravery, he's the one whose days are numbered.

The best surprise is that God is all over this book. Who else could have gotten this Jewish girl married to the king of a land where Jews were hated? Who else could play such a good joke on a creep like Haman?

I like your surprises, Lord. Please be in my life like you were in Esther's. Amen.

God Hopes

"Get up."
—Matthew 17:7

It's like watching funny home videos. When the dad stands behind his kid to teach him to swing the bat, you know that the dad will get hit instead of the baseball. When the bride's grandfather gets up on the table to dance, you know he'll come crashing down to the floor. If we're lucky, he'll end up with his face in the cake too.

It's the same with Judah. Once this kingdom decided to try life without organized religion, out from under God's control, they came crashing down hard.

But God wouldn't leave them there. Isaiah told them there would be a day when God would pick them up and wipe the cake off their faces.

God was talking about Jesus. And it's Jesus who picks you up when you do stupid stuff too.

Pick me up when I fall, Lord. Amen.

G-O-D and S-E-X

Why Do You Care?

So God created humankind in his image, in the image of God he
created them; male and female he created them.
—Genesis 1:27

Why does God meddle in our Mondays through Saturdays? As
long as we worship regularly and try to be good Christians, why
should God care whether we take a little hit of this or a little
smoke of that? Why would God care if we had a little fun?

God cares because God loves us. When God created us, we were
created in God's image. God cares about us so much that God
sent Jesus to save us from ourselves! God doesn't want us to
roll unthinkingly from one bed to another or to get hooked on a
chemical illusion of joy. God loves us so much that God wants the
best for us.

*God, save me from myself so that I can live what you desire for
me. Amen.*

What's the Minimum Age?

And the man and his wife were both naked, and were not ashamed.
—Genesis 2:25

How old do you have to be before having sex? It's not like voting, with a legal age requirement. Whether you're ready or not depends on a lot of factors that are difficult to put into numbers.

God's biblical plan for human relationships places faithful sexual intimacy within marriage. Some people rush into marriage because they want to experience sex and believe they have to be married. No one wants to deal with divorce, unplanned pregnancy, STDs, or emotional pain, but it's hard to wait.

God has placed sexual intimacy in long-term committed relationships for a reason—to guard our hearts and bodies until we have the maturity and trust needed for such a relationship. Waiting will be worth it.

God, help me to wait until I'm ready. Amen.

Sin Is Sin

"Let anyone among you who is without sin
be the first to throw a stone at her."
—John 8:7b

A woman in Jesus' time is caught in the act of adultery. A mob is preparing to carry out the usual punishment: death by stoning. Rather than joining the mob, Jesus confronts the crowd and sets up a challenge: someone who is sinless can be the first to throw a stone.

We tend to rank sins—thinking trespassing is less of a sin than adultery, for example. But sin is sin. All have sinned. None of us could cast the first stone. But we can all be grateful for the huge gift of forgiveness that we receive from God.

God, help me to accept your forgiveness and turn from my sin. Amen.

Steamy Stories from the Bible

Let him kiss me with the kisses of his mouth!
—Song of Solomon 1:2

Some people think of the Bible as a stuffy book of rules that forbids us to experience anything good. Well, that's all wrong. We can find intrigue, mystery, history, poetry, adventure, visions, wisdom, and romance in the Bible. We have to really read the Bible to find all these things. The steamiest Bible story might be plopped down in the middle of a boring description of a king's reign!

For instance, which king had a good man killed so he could take the man's wife? (Read 2 Samuel 11.) Who danced so seductively that a ruler said he would promise her *anything?* (Read Mark 6:14-29.) Who was arrested when he resisted the flirtations of a government official's wife? (Read Genesis 39.)

God, help me to learn more about you from the interesting stories in the Bible. Amen.

Let's Talk about Sex

Therefore a man leaves his father and his mother
and clings to his wife, and they become one flesh.
—Genesis 2:24

Years ago, people talked about sex being dirty or bad. Young people heard parents talk about sex in such a negative light (to keep them from having sex before marriage), that they couldn't imagine sex having any place in a marriage relationship!

The message today is a little different. Sex is best shared by people who trust each other completely, know each other intimately, and are committed to each other for life. Because sex is such a special commitment, people are encouraged to wait until marriage.

God, help me to sort out all the mixed messages about sex. Amen.

The God Part's Connected to the Sex Drive

I am my beloved's, and his desire is for me.
—Song of Solomon 7:10

The Song of Solomon is an extended love poem, presumably written for or by King Solomon. We don't know the details of the story, but this book of the Bible centers around the sexual attraction between two lovers.

When we make a decision based on our sex drive, can we separate our spiritual self from that experience? Well . . . no. We can't compartmentalize our lives, even if we want to. Every part of us is intertwined with every other part. We can't make a decision in one area that doesn't affect the rest. All of our desires, feelings, and hopes are connected in our hearts, minds, and souls.

God, help me to see all the parts of my life as connected to each other. Amen.

Baby Mama Drama

Hagar bore Abram a son. . . .
—Genesis 16:15

God said, "No, but your wife Sarah shall bear you a son."
—Genesis 17:19

God promised Abraham he would be the father of many nations. As Abraham grew older, he doubted God's words, so he made a back-up plan. Sarah, his wife, gave him permission to have a child with her slave girl, Hagar. Afterwards, things got so tense that Hagar ran away to the wilderness (Genesis 16:6). This part of the story is difficult for us to hear.

Remember, God had already made a covenant with Abraham. God had already told Abraham the plan—that Abraham and Sarah would have a child together to fulfill God's promise for the many generations to come. No matter how hard it was for Abraham and Sarah to believe in that covenant, God was ready to fulfill it.

God, thanks for fulfilling your promise to Abraham. Help me trust your promises. Amen.

A Church Is a Church: A Church by Any Other Name Is Still a Church

Let's try this one:
A.A.A.A. Church.

Aw, Dad, do we have to go to a public building for worship in the company of our like-minded fellow Christians today?
BUSH

What Is Church?

For as in one body we have many members, and not all the members
have the same function, so we, who are many, are one body in Christ,
and individually we are members one of another.
—Romans 12:4-5

To be very honest, we are turned off by unusual people in church
(for example, people who have different political viewpoints
than us or talk too much or disagree with every good idea that
we have). But in his letter to the Romans, Paul says that we are
"members one of another" in the body of Christ, which is the
church. Though we are individuals, we are tied together in the
family of the church. Like it or not, it's true.

God gives us church relationships to bring us support, comfort,
and encouragement. We can speak the truth in love, disagree with
our fellow Christians, and still rely on each other in times of need.

God, help our church members to support one another. Amen.

Let It Be a City of Love

Let your light shine before others.
—Matthew 5:16

Every day, whether or not we realize it, we choose how we will represent Jesus to others. We do this in the way we talk and the way we act, in the things we do and the things we don't do.

What if people saw us showing real love to others? What if we let our lights shine?

Jesus, Light of the World, help me to let my light shine. Amen.

Talk the Talk, but also Walk the Walk

For just as the body without the spirit is dead,
so faith without works is also dead.
—James 2:26

Sometimes we say one thing, but act out another. We say we love all people, but treat busboys as though they're trash. We say that God created the world, but throw garbage out the car window. We say Jesus is the Prince of Peace, but fight over every little church decision.

What about you? Where are you talking the talk, but not walking the walk? In the way you treat people? The way you treat yourself? Choices you have made? Things done or left undone?

The good news is that God allows U-turns. There is always room for a change in action, a change in behavior. And God can help you make that change.

God of U-turns, show me how to live what I believe. Amen.

Give It Up

He called to the crowd with his disciples, and said to them,
"If any want to become my followers, let them deny
themselves and take up their cross and follow me."
—Mark 8:34

Sometimes the church makes it a piece of cake to follow Jesus: Do what you want (or not); commit to something (if you really feel like it); show up (if you have nothing better to do). This faith is not a commitment, it's a convenient add-on (if you feel like it).

Jesus doesn't offer an easy, no-purchase-necessary, money-back-guarantee kind of faith. Jesus calls us to sacrifice on behalf of our neighbors and for the sake of the gospel. We must say yes to some things and no to others. This is what it means to take up our cross and follow Jesus.

God, help me to follow you, no matter how hard it gets. Amen.

I'm looking for a church that will lead me to lay down in greener pastures.

The Grass Is Always Greener

The Lord is my shepherd, I shall not want. He makes me lie down in green pastures; he leads me beside still waters; he restores my soul.
—Psalm 23:1–3

Earthly blessings, eternal life, forgiveness of sins—what more could you ask for? Green pastures, still waters, soul restoration—God can provide it all! How could anyone turn this down?

Well, green pastures and still waters sound appealing, but sometimes it's hard to be part of the church. You deal with different types of people. You have to sacrifice and lose things that are important to you. You have to follow the directions of a God you cannot see.

Being part of the church isn't easy, but the rewards are certainly priceless.

God, thanks for all your great gifts, including the gift of the church. Help me to be more faithful. Amen.

Learning from the Sins of the Past

I hate, I despise your festivals, and I take no delight
in your solemn assemblies.
—Amos 5:21

The Inquisition. The Crusades. The Holocaust. The settling of the
Americas. Many brutalities have been perpetrated in the name
of the church. A lot of hate and violence has been spread in the
name of Christ. It can make us embarrassed to even be Christians.

Sometimes we need to be truth-tellers and acknowledge where our
church has erred. We were too slow to speak out against slavery.
We remained quiet too long when Jews were being carried off to
concentration camps. Perhaps knowing these things and regretting
them will help us to act more quickly the next time we observe
injustice.

*God, forgive us when we go astray. Help us to fight against
injustice. Amen.*

Questions to Ask God Sometime

Dead Man Walking

Then he began to teach them that the Son of Man must undergo
great suffering, and be rejected by the elders, the chief priests,
and the scribes, and be killed, and after three days rise again.
—Mark 8:31

How many times have you seen a dead guy walking down the
road? The disciples had seen Jesus hanging on the cross a few
days earlier. He was dead, completely dead. Usually dead guys
stay dead, so you have to cut the disciples some slack if they
seemed confused.

Sure, Jesus had mentioned this might happen. A secret code
would have been helpful. A little proof is nice, but then, that
doesn't leave much room for faith, does it?

It's more subtle now, but Jesus continues to meet us on the road
of life. Would you know him if you saw him?

*Lord, in our daily encounters with you, help us to believe. Remind
us that you walk with us, even if you have to step on our toes
occasionally. Amen.*

Is This a Hook, Line, and Sinker Situation?

[Jesus] said to them, "Follow me, and I will make you fish for people."
—Matthew 4:19

What comes to mind when you see a large pile of fish? Good eats? Smelly gull treats? Folks who fished for a living a couple thousand years ago (long before hot showers and soap-on-a-rope) probably didn't have the best aroma. Okay, at the end of a day's work, they probably stunk. Fishing was hard, sweaty work with long hours and low pay.

So why would Jesus—God's own Son—head straight for the shore to find his first disciples? Why not do a few miracles to recruit religious leaders or the rich and powerful? Jesus' actions spoke volumes: he used everyday folks to accomplish amazing things. He still does.

Jesus, you call ordinary people to do extraordinary work. Toss us a net and teach us to fish, that your catch may continue. Amen.

Can You Define "Good"?

For I am convinced that neither death, nor life, nor angels, nor rulers,
nor things present, nor things to come, nor powers, nor height,
nor depth, nor anything else in all creation, will be able
to separate us from the love of God in Christ Jesus our Lord.
—Romans 8:38-39

Have you ever been to church during Holy Week, the week before Easter? Chances are the pews aren't packed. Sometimes people would rather just show up on Easter. That other stuff is too depressing.

Ever wonder why they call it "Good" Friday? What's so good about Jesus kicking the bucket on that nasty cross? If the story stopped there, it wouldn't be so good at all. But his death is an important first half of a great story. He died for us and then he knocked the wind out of sin and death a few days later. And that is eternally good.

God, we don't always get it, but we know that it is good. Thank you for Jesus, who died for us and lives for us too. Amen.

It's a Miracle . . . Right?

Augustin's wife is getting better, and so is Margaret Mochinn,
whose escape from death seems an absolute miracle. On the other
hand, we have lost five pigs, which is very disagreeable; however,
I hope the plague will accept them as our full contribution.
—Martin Luther

We've all done it. If Jesus loves us, wouldn't he want us to get an
"A" on a test? Shouldn't he miraculously turn that red light green
when we're running late? If you've been good, it seems like he
owes you one. But Jesus and Santa Claus aren't the same guy, not
even cousins.

Do we need miracles to believe in God? Probably not, but
honestly, some days a little reminder for us and proof for the
world might bolster the whole operation.

*God, help me to appreciate your everyday miracles and to save my
prayers for the good stuff. Amen.*

Can God Still Do Plagues?

Moses said to God, "Who am I that I should go to Pharaoh,
and bring the Israelites out of Egypt?"
—Exodus 3:11

Did you ever sport one of the "What Would Jesus Do?" bracelets?
Nice fad, but maybe bringing it down a level and asking what
Moses would do might be a better question to wrap around your
wrist. After all, you're not God, but you might not be so different
from Moses.

Moses stuttered. He balked when God gave him an important
job to do. He was also a murderer, but that's another story. What
would Moses do? He'd probably whine and complain, then take a
good crack at what God asked him to do. He'd probably stumble a
few times, but remain faithful. Not a bad role model at all.

*God, throughout the ages, you've put average folks to good use.
Help me to follow in that path. Amen.*

Does the Vineyard Have Sunblock?

Blessed is that slave whom his master will find
at work when he arrives. Truly I tell you, he will put
that one in charge of all his possessions.
—Luke 12:43-44

Is God fair? Thankfully, no. If God ruled fairly and everyone got what he or she deserved, humanity would be in a world of hurt. God cuts us a break on the fairness, but God calls us to take good care of others in return.

Sometimes that work will almost break your back, but God wants us to be busy bees giving attention to others and the world. Stewardship of God's kingdom is hard work, but the reward is sweet.

God, it's hot down here. Please send some help, so the harvest in your vineyard will overflow. Amen.

The 10, 15, 20, 25 Commandments

Moses is dead.
—Martin Luther

Sometimes the commandments seem too heavy for us. So why not narrow them down to 8? Why not 6 for that matter? Better yet, let's knock it down to the two easiest commandments.

Too bad. We'd still blow it. But that's good news, really. Because once we've busted the commandments, all that's left for us is Jesus.

The commandments count—all 10 of them—no matter how difficult they are. But we've got something better than whittling them down. We have Christ. Moses is dead. Jesus is alive; he offers forgiveness and he gives us his goodness.

Dear Jesus, these commandments are tough. But you are tougher. Thanks for being on my side. Amen.

How do we honor our mother and father when we have a babysitter?
BUSH

Was there a 4 1/2th Commandment?

We should fear and love God, and so we should not despise
our parents and superiors, nor provoke them to anger,
but honor, serve, obey, love, and esteem them.
—Martin Luther

Honor sounds like something you do as you salute, but it doesn't have to be so rigid. Honoring your parents or whoever was responsible for your upbringing is part of all that you do. Your speech and conduct when you are away from your family either brings honor upon them or strips it away.

And you thought no one was watching.

God, there's enough honor for all the folks who parent us, full time and sometimes. Help us to spread it thick. Amen.

Can You Please Pass Lot's Wife?

Somewhere on earth there must still be some godly people,
or else God would not grant us so many blessings!
—Martin Luther

All she did was look back. Everyone looks back occasionally. Sometimes a backward glance helps you figure out where you're going. But in giving in to her urge to look back at Sodom, she disobeyed God. Lot's wife, whose name isn't in the Bible, only had one chance to disobey.

But her husband, Lot, took advantage of multiple opportunities to violate God's commands. When the crowd assembled at Lot's door to abuse God's messengers hiding in the house, Lot offered his daughters to be plundered instead. His sins were potent and difficult to leave behind, yet God spared Lot when Sodom was destroyed.

God, thanks for giving me second chances. Amen.

Can You Define "Share"?

We should fear and love God, and so we should not rob our neighbor
of his money or property, nor bring them into our possession
by dishonest trade or by dealing in shoddy wares, but help him
to improve and protect his income and property.
—Martin Luther

Okay, maybe you don't have to share everything. After all, if someone needed underwear, you wouldn't peel yours off and hand it over. Instead, you could happily truck down to the store to buy that person his or her own brand new pair.

Possessions aren't bad in themselves, but they can easily become obstacles to faith. After our daily needs are provided for, belongings are low on the list of God's priorities. Except for you, Teddy.

God, help me to love you, my family, my friends, and my neighbors more than the stuff around me. Amen.

Peculiarities

The Good Book worm

Tong in Cheek

Do you not know that you are God's temple
and that God's Spirit dwells in you?
—1 Corinthians 3:16

The gifts of the Holy Spirit are varied and many. And okay, some are just plain bizarre. Speaking in tongs? Why not? There are stranger things attributed to the Spirit. If it spreads the good news to a few of the world's grillers, it's done some good. Tong away.

God, may your Spirit live in me and may I never evict it. Amen.

It's 10:00 P.M.
Do You Know Where Your Kids Are?

Jesus said to him, "Simon son of John, do you love me?"
He said to him, "Yes, Lord; you know that I love you."
Jesus said to him, "Tend my sheep."
—John 21:16

Jesus could have looked sharp on a throne, but there isn't any supporting evidence that he spent any time sitting on one. He didn't fritter away his years on earth fawning over the wealthy and powerful.

But folks still might have been quick to hitch their wagons to his whole operation if he hadn't referred to himself as a shepherd so much. This conveyed a whole new way of bringing in those who are lost, caring for those who are weak, even carrying those who are broken.

It was a little too down-to-earth.

Lord, hook us with your staff when we're lost. Teach us to care for the rest of the flock too. Amen.

See the Future (and the Past)

Out of the depths I cry to you; O Father, hear me calling. Incline your ear to my distress in spite of my rebelling. Do not regard my sinful deeds. Send me the grace my spirit needs; without it I am nothing.
—Martin Luther

Have you ever wished for a clear answer from God about a big dilemma or decision? Maybe you've tried this approach: You dust off the Bible and set it in front of you, shut your eyes, flip the Bible open, then place your finger on a sentence on a randomly opened page. Did you find the answer to your dilemma? Was God moving the pages and your hand?

A better approach might be opening your eyes and reading the psalms. Sometimes it's nice to know you're not alone.

God, open my eyes and my Bible. Show me that I'm not in this alone. Amen.

I'll Have the Recommended Daily Amount of Grace, Please

[Jesus] has snatched us, poor lost creatures, from the jaws of hell, won us, made us free, and restored us to the Father's favor and grace.
—Martin Luther

Start your stopwatch. Don't sin. Really, stop. Okay, how long did you last?

News flash: humans sin and can't stop. Sure, we can whittle things down to a manageable count, but as soon as we start doing really well, we probably start judging others and, whoops, we sinned again.

But that's not the end of the story. Jesus paid the bill in full. He showed up on earth knowing that we were a bunch of crazy sinners and he loved us anyway. He loved us enough to die on that nasty cross, stomped out death, and lived to tell about it.

God, help us to go and sin no more and then go and sin no more again. . . . Thanks for the clean slates. Amen.

Somebody Needs a Sabbath

We keep holy days so that people may have time and opportunity, which otherwise would not be available, to participate in public worship, that is, that they may assemble to hear and discuss God's Word and then praise God with song and prayer.
—Martin Luther

Given a choice between plowing a field behind a couple of oxen or going to church, which would you select? Right, that's an easy question. But what if the choice was going to church or hanging out at the mall, surfing the Web, and text messaging the day away? Whatever your thing, your brain needs a break.

Sabbath doesn't mean sitting in a chair all day staring at the walls, but it is taking leave from the everyday. Think of Sabbath as a holiday for your soul that keeps God from being choked out by all the other stuff. Give it up for God—and for you.

God, slow me down and teach me to keep a Sabbath. It's a date— with you. Amen.

This one is a little Psalm I wrote one day when I was lying by some still waters.
DAVID
Thru Thurs.

Righteous Dude

The Lord is righteous; he loves righteous deeds.
—Psalm 11:7

If the psalms mean nothing more to you than elevator music, then something has gone terribly wrong. Psalms of praise should be a little bit country, a little bit rock and roll, but never boring. The psalms aren't commenting on dinner; they're celebrating God the Creator!

The lives of the psalm writers weren't easy, but nonetheless, they found inspiration knowing that God walked with them through all their days. When cruising through dark valleys, God doesn't slap you on the back and say, "See you on the other side." God remains through it all. That's something to sing about.

God, thanks for the voices in the psalms. Throw some still waters my way any time. Amen.

May I Offer You an Hors D'oeuvre before the Meal?

Then the king gave the command, and Daniel was brought and thrown into the den of lions. The king said to Daniel, "May your God, whom you faithfully serve, deliver you!"
—Daniel 6:16

Ripped away from his home in Jerusalem and taken captive many years before, Daniel adjusted to life as a foreigner except for one snag—his faith in God. The Babylonians surrounding him demanded he cease worshiping and praying to God. But Daniel wouldn't bend, and apparently he couldn't be broken, either.

Jealous people conspired to have Daniel thrown into a lions' den. But when the stone was rolled away the next day, the king found Daniel safe and sound—and all his tasty limbs too.

God, help me to remain strong and sturdy when others try to chop away at my faith. Keep the lions at bay today. Amen.

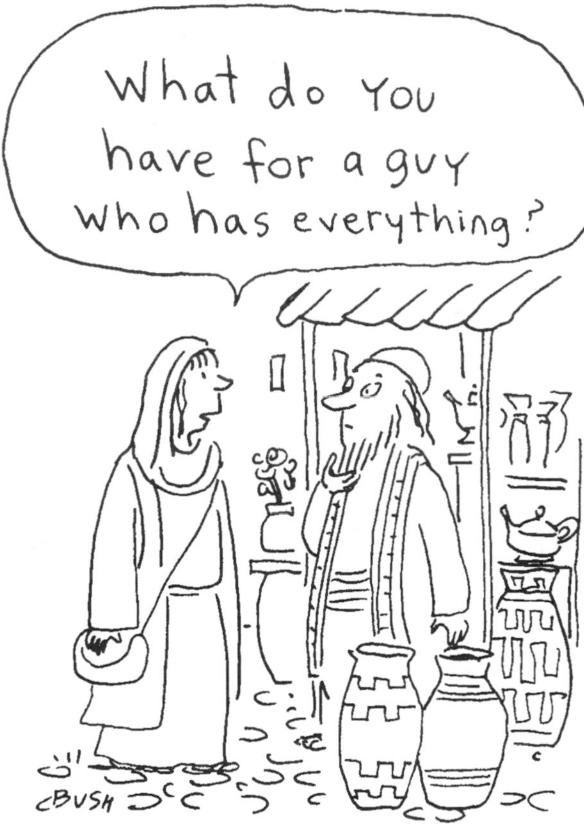
What do You have for a guy who has everything?
BUSH

How about a Clue?

King Solomon made two hundred large shields of beaten gold;
six hundred shekels of gold went into each large shield.
—1 Kings 10:16

There's having everything and then there's King Solomon,
who made the old "everything" look pitiful. Solomon built
an enormous temple to worship God, and then made his own
palace twice as large. Coincidence? Solomon was first known
for wisdom, but eventually he was ordering up worthless shields
made of gold. (Note to Solomon: gold is a soft metal.) But
perhaps his most excessive move was in marriage. He married
seven hundred foreign wives and secured another three hundred
mistresses, defying God's command a thousand times.

In spite of this excessive lifestyle, God worked through Solomon.
That's because God is excessive too—in love and forgiveness.

Lord, let my only excess be that of love. Amen.

Stop, You're Killing Me!

Then King David went in and sat before the LORD, and said, "Who am I, O Lord GOD, and what is my house, that you have brought me thus far?"
—2 Samuel 7:18

Who's watching the sheep, David? The young man destined for a grand future left the flock to see who was going to take on the giant Philistine, Goliath. Somehow David got recruited for the job and bowled down the big guy with one fast rock.

It was an ironic start for a king who would travel a rocky road. God blessed Israel through David, often in spite of his actions, not because of them. In the end, David committed murder and adultery, but despite this, God continued the covenant through him.

God, you used David for good things despite his imperfections. There must be a place for me too. Amen.

You're Not the Boss of Me

In those days there was no king in Israel;
all the people did what was right in their own eyes.
—Judges 21:25

No, not *those* kind of judges. The Old Testament judges were more like rulers. No, not *those* kind of rulers. More like the kind God might use as a reminder when folks forgot how to live.

About the time the Israelites turned away from God, they opened the door for foreign invaders to show up. Judges defended the people (sometimes against themselves) with military might. Like the calvary, in came the judges to liberate the people and kick out the invaders.

What would judges tell us today?

God, are there judges in our midst? Bring us back when we go too far. Amen.

Why Can't You Pray Nice with Your Sister?

If your faith and trust are right, then your God is the true God. . . .
For these two belong together, faith and God. That to which
your heart clings and entrusts itself, is, I say, really your God.
—Martin Luther

Faith is this strange combination of private, yet very public. You can believe alone, worship alone, pray alone, but you can't live out your faith alone.

People often speak of faith as if it were (like politics) not to be discussed in polite company. They see it as a very secret thing between one's God and one's soul. But faith ultimately shows itself publicly through lives like yours.

Maybe it would be more accurate to declare that belief is private, but faith is public—and alive in the world.

God, help us to share our faith with everyone in the world, even the ones we can't stand. Amen.

I Am the Lord Your God, So Listen Up!

Did You Run Out of Adults?

Now the Lord came and stood there, calling as before, "Samuel!
Samuel!" And Samuel said, "Speak, for your servant is listening."
—1 Samuel 3:10

God called a little scrapper named Samuel into the work of
prophecy. It wasn't a job for wimps. Sam might not have been
able to spell them, but he had to speak some hard truths, even to
the guy who raised him.

Think you're too young to do much good for God? Think again.

*God, you've always done your work through unlikely people, and
even through kids. Here I am, Lord. Your servant is listening.
Amen.*

274 / The Funny Shape of Faith

Exactly How Near?

For just as we, through the faith of our Master, are Christ's brethren,
and are kings and priests, so are we all through Christ also prophets.
—Martin Luther

A prophet is slapped with an unpopular assignment: to warn
people of their wrongdoing and tell them to clean up their
collective acts. You couldn't give a job like that away!

Throughout the ages, God has spoken through the prophets. For
just as long, prophets have been mocked, ridiculed, beat up, and
tossed out. It's never a popular job, but it's a necessary one to
bring God's people back in line. God says listen up and sometimes
even speak up.

*God, help me to listen to the voice of the prophets and to
sometimes be that voice too, even when it is unpopular. Amen.*

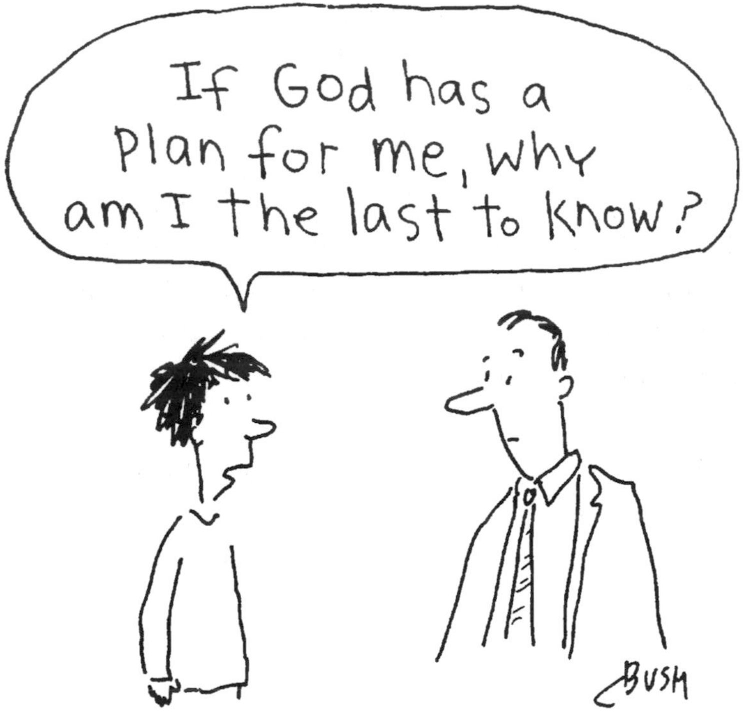
If God has a plan for me, why am I the last to know?
BUSH

Will It Have a Happy Ending?

"There is hope for your future," says the Lord.
—Jeremiah 31:17

God's plans for the Israelites involved hope, promise, and a Savior.

Sometimes it might seem to us like the world is on autopilot and God's plan is, "Let's see how this one goes," or it might seem like God is playing a giant game of chess that hopefully will make sense when it's finished. Then again, maybe God's plan wouldn't be so great if we could comprehend it.

Hello, God. Offer me glimpses of your plan for my life and help me to live it. Amen.

Look Out Below!

And [Jesus] sighed deeply in his spirit and said,
"Why does this generation ask for a sign? Truly I tell you,
no sign will be given to this generation."
—Mark 8:12

Have you ever prayed for a sign? We believe by faith and not by sight, but an occasional sign sure couldn't hurt. The Bible tells us two things about signs:

1. God sometimes offered signs expressing warnings or approval.

2. Jesus seemed annoyed by requests for a sign.

Maybe the presence of Jesus should have been sign enough for the people of his time. If they got another sign, would it matter?

The challenge then of a sign from God might be both seeing it and following it.

God, a sign from you from time to time would be nice, but help me to carry on faithfully even without one. Amen.

Noah's Ark
Couples Cruise
40 day
Minimum.

cBUSH

The Rainbow Connection

God said, "This is the sign of the covenant that I make
between me and you and every living creature
that is with you, for all future generations."
—Genesis 9:12

When the ark landed on solid ground, God made a covenant with Noah. Actually, God's covenant with Noah extended to every generation that followed Noah *and* every living creature and animal. God promised to never again flood the earth. As a sign of God's covenant, God placed the rainbow in the clouds.

God gives this promise to you too. You are an heir of the covenant that God made with Noah. You may not have been on the "Noah's Ark Couples Cruise," but you are washed by saving waters as well.

God, thank you for giving us the rainbow as a sign of your love and as a sign of your covenant with us. Amen.

Sometimes a Ladder Is Just a Ladder

Then Jacob woke from his sleep and said,
"Surely the Lᴏʀᴅ is in this place—and I did not know it!"
—Genesis 28:16

Sometimes a ladder is just a ladder, but God has often used dreams to speak to believers (and a few non-believers too). Does this mean you should skip worship and sleep in so you're ready for any message God sends your way? Well, that argument just might buy you a few extra minutes. Use it sparingly, of course, since it can be reversed when negotiating lights out!

God speaks to us today in many ways. And God just might be speaking to you. Take time to listen.

Lord, make my mind still and open to your message. Remind me that surely you are in this place. Amen.

Can You Hear Me Now?

The Word of God is the true holy thing above all holy things.
—Martin Luther

It's hard to hear anything when we're not listening.

Maybe it wasn't chirping on the cell phone, but who hasn't doodled on a sermon note, caught up with the latest gossip, counted all the vowels in the bulletin, or balanced the checkbook in the pew? Some preachers are better than others, but they are all doing their best to speak the Word of God to those who will heed it.

Can you heed me now?

God, help us to listen to your Word. Make it real and alive in our lives. Amen.

So That's How It Started

Now to him who by the power at work within us is able to accomplish
abundantly far more than all we can ask or imagine, to him be glory in
the church and in Christ Jesus to all generations, forever and ever.
—Ephesians 3:20-21

The church, with all its imperfections and strange traditions,
stands as a visible sign of Christ's remaining presence on earth.
And here's the thing: The church isn't the pews or the building or
even the pastor. The people are the church. Others come to know
God in part through the church, through people like you.

Here's the church, here's the steeple, open the door, and see all of
God's people. Is that you near the back?

*God, build up your church and bulk us up to be the big body of
Christ on earth so everyone can smile to know your love. Amen.*

What's "Plan B"?

I will make them one nation in the land, on the mountains of Israel;
and one king shall be king over them all. Never again shall they be
two nations, and never again shall they be divided into two kingdoms.
—Ezekiel 37:22

Israel separated into two nations. Just two? What's the big deal about that? Has anyone kept track of how many splits there have been in Christianity?

This split was a big deal and here's why. After the country fell apart, everyone's focus turned to getting life back to the way it used to be—back to "the good old days." The problem was, the old days were gone . . . forever.

Life changes. You can learn to adapt or spend your whole life pointlessly trying to turn it into what it was before. At some point we may have to punt and remember that God works in mysterious ways, even when we don't get it.

God, sometimes it would be nice to know what's going on. When your plans confuse me, remind me that you are God and you are wise. Amen.

That's So Last Millennium

At whatever time God's Word is taught, preached, heard,
read, or pondered, there the person, the day, and the work
are sanctified by it, not on account of the external work
but on account of the Word which makes us all saints.
—Martin Luther

Roll your eyes if you've ever thought your parents were clueless.
Refocus those eyes, then nod your head if you've ever claimed the
Bible is boring. Here's the secret: your parents probably believed
the older generation was clueless, just as your kids will someday
believe you to be. And the Bible can be a snoozer in parts, but
it's also a rocking, raunchy PG-13 book because it's written about
humans like you.

The details of each generation appear different, but the struggles
of humanity remain pretty much the same. It's all in there.

*God, remind me to crack open the Bible. When I do, help me see
myself and my place as one of your people. Amen.*

Surprising Savior Stuff

Help that Helps

"Go and learn what this means, 'I desire mercy, not sacrifice.'
For I have come to call not the righteous but sinners."
—Matthew 9:13

People show up at church not knowing what is wrong with their lives, seeking healing and wholeness and new life. How often are they met by someone telling them what they already know and offering simple solutions to complex problems: "You are a sinner. Stop sinning! And by the way, you must wear shoes and appropriate dress here in THIS church. Didn't you know?"

Jesus shows us a better way. Take care of the person and the pain first. God's laws have an order to them: mercy before sacrifice, love before the law.

Dear God, help us to offer the help people need. Use us to spread your message of hope and healing for the world. Amen.

When I Grow Up . . .

Philip found Nathanael and said to him, "We have found him
about whom Moses in the law and also the prophets wrote,
Jesus son of Joseph from Nazareth."
—John 1:45

Whether baseball, football, or rock 'n' roll, we give our heroes
places in a hall of fame. What do you know about the Faith Hall
of Fame in your congregation? What does it take to have a place
there? How might ordinary folks be encouraged by a visit?

When we recognize the contributions of those who have come
before us, we are encouraged to make our own contributions and
follow faithfully.

*Dear God, you call us to lives of faith. Inspire us to follow Jesus.
Amen.*

Hmm . . . What Will It Take?

"Give us this day our daily bread."
—Matthew 6:11

Our God of immeasurable abundance hears us and responds. When we are hungry, God responds with bread of life. When we are thirsty, God responds with living water. Whatever our need, God responds. This we pray for. This we receive. Manna in the desert. Food on a hill. Mercy and love for the living we will do this day.

All this is not just to provide us with what we need. God does all this so we will know and be known and will be in an ongoing relationship with the restless soul-saving Creator of the universe. WOW.

Dear God of manna and quail, fish and loaves, bread and wine: feed us, restore us, and call us your own. Now and forever. Amen.

This Way and That

Jesus was led up by the Spirit into the wilderness
to be tempted by the devil.
—Matthew 4:1

Temptations come in all sizes and shapes, colors and sounds. Temptation happens when the tempter takes any good thing and twists it into something that steals life. Food is good, but too little or too much can be unhealthy. Games are good, but not all night when you have finals in the morning.

We live complex lives in a complex world. Some are tempted to give simple answers that work once and get tossed. There are temptations at church too—temptations to hold onto the gifts we're given, temptations to hoard our resources to secure our own future, temptations to distrust outsiders.

Over and over we are called by God back into Scripture, back into trusting God's goodness, back to leading lives of faith.

Lead us not into temptation, Lord. Help us see your goodness at work in the small things. Amen.

The sign on the door reads: "AWAY IN THE MANGER BE BACK IN 10."

Manger Break

But this is the covenant that I will make with the house of Israel after those days, says the Lord: I will put my law within them, and I will write it on their hearts; and I will be their God, and they shall be my people.

—Jeremiah 31:33

God is full of surprises—like the surprise of the Christ-child, the surprise of a law written on our hearts, the surprise of the Holy Spirit active in our world each day.

Look for surprises. Expect them. You will see signs all around testifying to God's goodness and love for the world. The surprise of the signs is that God is not always where we would think to look, but always working out new ways to get us to connect with grace and love. Look at the world with eyes of faith and see God's love surrounding us all.

Baby Jesus, thank you for the gift and surprise of your birth, for the sake of the whole world. Amen.

They came bearing gold, frankincense, and diapers.

What Do You Really Need, Jesus?

"Is there anyone among you who,
if your child asks for bread, will give a stone?"
—Matthew 7:9

Being honored by kings is important, but doesn't Baby Jesus need diapers? Being honored by other nations and empires is important, but doesn't Jesus need our hearts?

What would you bring to the baby if you were one of the kings? What can you give him today?

Dear Baby Jesus, help us make good decisions about what's important in our lives and in our relationship with you. Amen.

We Didn't Think Anybody Would Get Hurt!

Then they stoned Paul and dragged him out of the city,
supposing that he was dead.
—Acts 14:19

Turn on the TV or get the latest news feed and it's clear that this is a violent world. War, famine, and disease rage across the globe.

What is the cost of discipleship, the cost of following Jesus? On the battlefield, people take stands and die. In our communities or nations, we might take a stand and get arrested.

We follow Jesus who sacrificed his life for us. What are we willing to sacrifice for the sake of spreading the good news about him? Where do we draw the line?

God of all good things, help us to be a force for peace in the world. Show us and guide us and lead us into non-violent solutions to our problems. Amen.

What Are They Up To?

When he was at the table with them, he took bread, blessed
and broke it, and gave it to them. Then their eyes were opened,
and they recognized him; and he vanished from their sight.
—Luke 24:30-31

How can a roomful of people be fed by a cup and a loaf? Or for
that matter, how can a ragtag bunch of faithful people make a
church work?

We know that God works wonders with woefully meager
resources. That's one way we know it's God's good work! But
what we do in the church is often a mystery to the rest of the
world. Think of it, a thirty-three-year-old Jesus promises to be
with us whenever we have this meal, then is murdered by the
government and church leaders of his day. Two thousand years
later, we confess that Jesus is Lord and truly present in this meal.

And the rest of the world wonders, do we get a tip?

*Lord, the blessing of Jesus your Son is for the sake of the world. Help
us to be such a blessing that it is perfectly clear to everyone that the
world is a better place because of the followers of Jesus. Amen.*

Too Hot to Handle!

So those who welcomed his message were baptized,
and that day about three thousand persons were added.
—Acts 2:41

For good or for fear, resurrection power cannot be ignored. Three thousand people in Jerusalem, hearing about the risen Lord, are baptized on Pentecost day. The soldiers at Jesus' empty tomb, believing the worst, run for their lives.

We know of God's power over death. We know of God's love for the world. We know of God's forgiveness and mercy. We know of God's resurrection power.

This news is too hot to handle. Pass it on!

Risen Christ, fill us and the world with your resurrection power. Amen.

Wholly Spirit

"But the Advocate, the Holy Spirit, whom the Father
will send in my name, will teach you everything,
and remind you of all that I have said to you."
—John 14:26

God is not just what we think. God is wholly other and holy
other. God surprises us with simplicity and majesty, humility and
extravagance. We use the naming of God as Father, Son, and Holy
Spirit as a kind of shorthand for all the names and activity of God
in our world.

We're tempted to laugh at the girl in the cartoon, with her silly
notion of the Holy Spirit. But don't all of our descriptions fall
short?

*Dear God, help us to know you as you know us, with hearts of
love. Amen.*

Well . . . That's Just Silly

The Holy and the Holey

Then Abraham fell on his face and laughed, and said to himself,
"Can a child be born to a man who is a hundred years old?
Can Sarah, who is ninety years old, bear a child?"
—Genesis 17:17

It's fun to look at the friar and the fryer and giggle.

When something is holy—not full of holes "holey," or completely there "wholly," but sacred and from God "holy," it brings a smile to our hearts. Sometimes when the holy breaks into our everyday world, it breaks through our preconceptions and helps us giggle a bit. It helps us remember that the world and everything in it are God's.

All things are possible with God. And God likes to play.

God of possibilities, help us see the holey as wholly holy. Help us to see your hand in our work. Help us to see your handiwork and to smile in our hearts. Amen.

Into the Great Wide Open

"And remember, I am with you always, to the end of the age."
—Matthew 28:20b

Trying out new things, going to places we've never been before, or trying out new ways of being friends with people are all things that can make us nervous and frightened.

There are times when we find ourselves in uncharted territory. At times like these, we can take comfort in Jesus' promise to be with us and look forward to the challenge that new adventures will bring.

God of adventure, thank you for each new day. Give us courage and keep our eyes open for new possibilities. Amen.

Hot Off the Press

[Paul and Silas] spoke the word of the Lord to [the jailer]
and to all who were in his house.
—Acts 16:32

The good news about Jesus was first spread by one person or group to another. The women left the empty tomb and told the disciples, who told others. Paul and Silas told their jailer and his household.

In Luther's day the Gutenberg press was the latest technology. God used it to spread a word of grace to the people. We are challenged to understand the gospel and use every means available to bring it to the ones who have yet to hear it. What are the technologies we use today to spread the good news? How can you help spread the good news with the technology you know?

Oh, and don't forget, an old-fashioned, face-to-face conversation still works too.

God of all, thank you for using the printing press and radio and TV and Internet to spread the gospel. Use us and all we know to help your kingdom come. Amen.

Give Me All the Options

Bind them as a sign on your hand, fix them as an emblem
on your forehead, and write them on the doorposts
of your house and on your gates.
—Deuteronomy 6:8-9

Our world loves options. We want to know all our choices and opportunities up front. We work hard to keep our options open. And we have a hard time taking commands from anyone.

Many people take the "I'll look them over and get back to you" attitude toward God and the commandments and God's people. But God, out of love for us, gives us commandments as a gift to nourish life. These commandments shape our relationship with God and with others. They are a critical foundation for abundant and joyful living.

God of Moses, deliver us from our selfishness and help us to see the life you offer. Help us to find life in your commands and strength in their boundaries. Help us to share the joy we find in you. Amen.

Waddaya Mean, You Don't Like My Coat?
(Joseph Was a Dweeb)

Then Joseph said to his brothers, "Come closer to me." And they came
closer. He said, "I am your brother, Joseph, whom you sold into Egypt.
And now do not be distressed, or angry with yourselves, because you
sold me here; for God sent me before you to preserve life."
—Genesis 45:4-5

Joseph is a show-off and a very obnoxious little brother. He's the
favorite son and gets away with all sorts of things that make his
brothers seethe with jealousy—and finally sell him into slavery.

As unlikely as it all sounds, Joseph keeps trusting in God and
becomes the instrument for God to save Israel from a seven-year
famine.

God's steadfast love is technicolor, amazing with surround sound!

*Lord of lords, your love for us is no less amazing than your love
for Joseph and his brothers. Bring a message of your love out of
the chaos of our lives. Bring good from the messes we make. For
the sake of your world, use us to do your work in the world. Amen.*

Spinning Sin

The man said, "The woman whom you gave to be with me,
she gave me fruit from the tree, and I ate."
—Genesis 3:12

We find it funny that Adam and Eve try to hide their forbidden
fruit episode from God. Of course, God will find out. And yet we
sin in all kinds of original ways, expecting never to be found out.
Sometimes we cover our sin with humor, sometimes we cover it
with excuses, sometimes we cover it by blaming others, but at
heart we always seem surprised that we are found out.

This is almost the oldest lesson in the book, and but it's still fresh
every day. Lord, have mercy.

*Lord, have mercy on us all. We sin. We fall short. We miss the
mark. Lord, have mercy on us all. Amen.*

What Does This Mean?

What would you prefer? Am I to come to you with a stick,
or with love in a spirit of gentleness?
—1 Corinthians 4:21

Love. How can a word that is sorely abused in the English language be central to understanding how God is with us? And yet, we speak of God's love at every chance we get, almost like the cheerleader in this cartoon.

Words fail us quite quickly, but song and dance and instruments and even the heavens declare the wonder of God's love. To love and be loved by God is the deepest longing of our hearts.

Lord, take us deep into the depths of your love, so that we might know what words will never quite capture—your love for us in Jesus Christ. Amen.

Trouble with a Capital "T"

"In the world you face persecution. But take courage;
I have conquered the world!"
—John 16:33b

The world expects you to be the same person tomorrow as you were yesterday. But Jesus meets you today and offers you new life. This can be more than a little threatening for the people—even people close to you—who expect you to remain the same.

Difficult choices and disappointed drinking buddies are often the result of finding new life in Christ.

Lord, as you give us new life, give us the strength to withstand the resistance of the world to our change. And grant us your peace. Amen.

Road Trip!

He called the crowd with his disciples, and said to them,
"If any want to become my followers, let them deny
themselves and take up their cross and follow me."
—Mark 8:34

The church is supposed to be on the move! Jesus is always out there with people who are poor and outcast, calling for the church to follow. But often the church moves at the speed of, well, the church—trying not to offend anyone, or make anyone uncomfortable, or stress anyone out.

What if we hop on and hang on and maybe bring a friend or two?

Jesus, help us to get on the church chariot with you and get moving. Give us a sense of urgency about your good news. Amen.

Where's the Drive-Through Lane?

I will put my law within them, and I will write it on their hearts;
and I will be their God, and they shall be my people.
—Jeremiah 31:33

People are used to getting things tailor-made to their tastes, and so there's the beginner's Bible, the teen Bible, the women's Bible, the new non-smoker's Bible, and the any-flavor-you-want Bible. You can spend a lot of time just window-shopping.

When it comes down to it, the Bible tells us about God's love for us in Jesus Christ. Maybe it's time to stop staring in the window. Maybe it's time to get a Bible to go.

Lord, help us not to window-shop for our faith. Lead us as we jump in and get going. Amen.

Tuned In

The word of the LORD came to me: Mortal, prophesy against the prophets of Israel who are prophesying; say to those who prophesy out of their own imagination: "Hear the word of the LORD!"
—Ezekiel 13:1-2

There are many voices in the world that want us to pay attention. When do we listen to God—really take time to quiet all the rest of the voices from school and home and friends and all THAT, and listen?

God's word is more than just another billboard, podcast, or instant message. It's the message of God's love for us in Jesus Christ. It's the greatest news ever! And we're more than just receivers. We're thinking, listening, responding followers—and spreaders—of this message.

Lord, get our attention. Help us to focus and listen and learn. Teach us, Lord, to have teachable hearts. Amen.

I am not now, nor ever was a false bear witness against my neighbor.
CBUSH

The Whole Truth, and Nothing But the Truth

And [the voice of the Lord] said, "Go and say to this people: 'Keep listening, but do not comprehend; keep looking, but do not understand.'"
—Isaiah 6:9

We tend to turn things around to suit ourselves. And we hate to admit it, but we can end up looking pretty ridiculous trying to talk our way out of things. Besides that, we can end up hurting other people and ourselves.

Knowing this about ourselves, our only hope is to confess to God what we have done and said, and throw ourselves on the mercy of the court.

Lord, give us ears to hear and hearts that understand your law and your love. Help us to plainly speak the truth in love. Amen.

It's Sacramentalish!

Down to the River to Pray

Oh sinner let's go down, let's go down, c'mon down,
Oh sinner let's go down, down to the river to pray.
—American Traditional

A day at the beach ends. Baptism is forever. A day at the beach
might get us a tan line. Baptism gets us a direct line to the heart
of God.

"You are my child," God says to you. "Today I choose you."

With the water and the word, you are washed of your sin and
come up new. You are made a child of God. God loves you
forever.

*God of amazing grace, thank you for your gift of grace, water, and
your word. I am yours forever. Amen.*

Walking Wet

"And now why do you delay? Get up, be baptized,
and have your sins washed away, calling on his name."
—Acts 22:16

One baptism lasts forever, because it is God's grace that saves us—and that never wears thin.

But we tend to stray and forget, get busy and go our own way. We need to be reminded of baptism and remember it daily. A super soaker helps, or a bowl of water on the way to worship, or making the sign of the cross.

Remember your baptism and walk wet all week.

God of water and the word, remind us and remember us when we stray. Amen.

Shortcuts to Grace

Morning by morning they gathered [the manna],
as much as each needed.
—Exodus 16:21

We have so much to do and so little time, we do everything we can to save time. But we haven't managed to change our basic DNA, which restricts and encourages us to do DAILY the things that are important in our lives. So we wash our hands daily, brush our teeth daily, go to sleep daily, and—if we want to learn it—practice the piano daily.

We are fed by God's word, but sometimes we'd like to put it away for another time. After all, how often do we really need it?

Well, how often do we eat?

God of daily life, help us to relish daily blessings and draw closer to you. Amen.

Can I Play Too?

See what love the Father has given us, that we should be called
children of God; and that is what we are.

—1 John 3:1

Baptism isn't just for children. It just makes us all children—
children of God.

No matter how old we are when it happens, in baptism we come
before God and receive grace upon grace. God's goodness comes
to us, washes us clean, and saves us from death and the devil.

Some of God's children are just a little taller and a little older,
that's all. Think of the church as a large pool with all kinds of
kids floating around.

*Dear Lord, you humble us with your goodness. Grant us grace to
embrace the people you send into our lives. Let us live lives of
thanks. Amen.*

Community

There is one body and one Spirit, just as you were called to the one hope of your calling, one Lord, one faith, one baptism, one God and Father of all, who is above all and through all and in all.
—Ephesians 4:4-6

We are called into community—a community of faith. We are forgiven and blessed to be a blessing in community—as we come to the Communion table. And we are sent out into the world in community—at least two by two, if not in groups of twelve or more.

Following Jesus in the world today is no job to do alone. It is the work of a hearty full-bodied community, centered on the full and hearty body of Christ.

God of all goodness, draw us close as you send us out—close to one another and close to you. Amen.

POST LAST SUPPER

True Presence Remembered

"This cup that is poured out for you is the new covenant in my blood."
—Luke 22:20

In Communion, are the bread and wine actually bread and wine anymore? Or are the bread and wine just bread and wine and nothing more than that?

In Communion, we are party to a mystery that defies definition. And yet, that mystery is a party that invites participation!

Christ is present. Christ goes with us. We remember where he found us and smile.

Rock of ages, you gather us, feed us, and send us for the sake of your world. Thank you. Amen.

Dunked

But when he saw many Pharisees and Sadducees coming for baptism, he said to them, "You brood of vipers! Who warned you to flee from the wrath to come? Bear fruit worthy of repentance."
—Matthew 3:7-8

Maybe sometimes we don't see baptism as the big deal it really is. And it's important to have others—a congregation—present.

But this "splash off" sounds like a media spectacle featuring two competitors: John the Baptist and Carl the Submerger. That puts the spotlight in the wrong place.

Baptism isn't a spectacle. It's a sacrament featuring God. That means the spotlight is on God's love and grace for us, each and every time.

And each of us can be part of the lighting crew.

God of Wonders, you are playful and holy, inspiring and challenging. Thank you for the love and grace you pour out in baptism. Amen.

The Spice of Life

As they were going along the road, they came to some water;
and the eunuch said, "Look, here is water!
What is to prevent me from being baptized?"
—Acts 8:36

God blesses the world and the church with a wonderful variety of people. But it doesn't always seem so wonderful to us. We sometimes think it's fine to welcome everyone into the church . . . well, except maybe for people we don't know, and people we can't stand (you know, the ones who really mess up).

But God's love is much bigger than ours. God's love is high and wide and deep enough for everyone, for the whole world. That includes people we don't know. And it includes people who really mess up.

And that includes us.

God of diversity, teach me to embrace the many facets of your imagination as you create all people in your image. Help me to share your grace with all. Amen.

Reservations

The Teacher asks, "Where is my guest room
where I may eat the Passover with my disciples?"
—Mark 14:14

Little did the disciples know what was going to happen at the Last Supper. Little do we know the possibilities God has in store for our lives.

God continues to gather and save us. Sometimes we have reservations about the table and the company. But God has our reservation secured. Trust that you'll be seated with Jesus and his friends. Get set for the adventure of a lifetime and a lifetime of adventure.

See you at the table of the Lord.

God of open arms, you welcome us and send us out. Help us to halt our hesitations and jump in, trusting in your love. Amen.